BODACIOUS

BODACIOUS

An AOL Insider Cracks the Code to
Outrageous Success for Women

MARY E. FOLEY
WITH
MARTHA I. FINNEY

AMACOM AMERICAN MANAGEMENT ASSOCIATION
New York • Atlanta • Chicago • Kansas City • San Francisco
Washington, D. C. • Brussels • Mexico City • Tokyo • Toronto

Special discounts on bulk quantities of AMACOM books are available to corpo-
rations, professional associations, and other organizations. For details, contact
Special Sales Department, AMACOM, a division of American Management
Association, 1601 Broadway, New York, NY 10019.
Tel.: 212-903-8316. Fax: 212-903-8083.
Web site: www.amacombooks.org

This publication is designed to provide accurate and authoritative information in
regard to the subject matter covered. It is sold with the understanding that the
publisher is not engaged in rendering legal, accounting, or other professional service. If legal advice or other expert assistance is required, the services of a competent professional person should be sought.

Library of Congress Cataloging-in-Publication Data

Foley, Mary, E., 1965–
   Bodacious : an AOL insider cracks the code to outrageous success for women
   / Mary E. Foley with Martha I. Finney.
      p. cm.
   Includes bibliographical references and index.
   ISBN 0-8144-7131-5 (hc)
      1. Women——Employment——United States. 2. Career developement——United
   States. 3. Vocational guidance for women——United States. 4. Success in busi
   ness——United States. 5. America Online (Online service) I. Finney, Martha I.
   II. Title.

HD6053 .F65 2001
650.1'082——dc21

                                                         2001034335

Printing number

10 9 8 7 6 5 4 3 2 1

Contents

PREFACE XI

ACKNOWLEDGMENTS XII

1   LIKE NOTHING YOU'VE EVER SEEN BEFORE 3

"Life's Short, Learn Fast" 3

"Some Computer Company" 5

Where the Boys Are 8

"Better I Should Suffer" 12

We're All Start-Ups 16

Somebody's Going to Want a Piece of You 21

This Is High-Wire Living 22

Why "Now"? 22

The Trip to Bodaciousness 24

This Is High-Performance Living 25

2   BODACIOUSNESS STARTS ON THE INSIDE 27

The Inside Story: Fourteen Bodacious Ways for
Career and Personal Power 31

Bodacious Women Make Their Self-Esteem Priority One . . 31

Bodacious Women Know Their Value Prevails 33

How to Make a Decision Like an Engineer 35

Bodacious Women Observe What's Happening but
Don't Jump to Conclusions 36

Bodacious Women Are Curious 38

Bodacious Women Trust Their Inner Voice 39

Bodacious Women Don't Take It Personally 41

How to Journal for Discovery 41

Bodacious Women Get Over It 46

Bodacious Women See Barriers as an Opportunity to
Do Things Differently 48

Bodacious Women Focus on What's Going Right 49

Bodacious Women Welcome Risk and Relish Change 50

Bodacious Women Know That "Gratitude" Only
Rhymes With "Servitude". 51

Bodacious Women Embrace Competition 52

Bodacious Women Cultivate Relationships for
Many Reasons 53

Bodacious Women Notice Moments of Magic
and Serendipity. 56

3 STAFF YOUR BODACIOUS START-UP SELF 59

How to Be a Great Client. 62

Your Mother Always Said to Choose Your
Friends Wisely 64

Strategies for Staffing Your Social Circles. 66

How to Be an Empire Builder. 78

The Three A's: Now Economy Ways to Leverage
Your Relationships 81

How to Be a Great Consultant 83

The Ten Things You Want Your Reputation to Say
About You. 87

4 BODACIOUS WOMEN TAKE A STAND. 91

Get Control Over What You Can Control 94

Why Bother?. 97

Don't Let This One Slide 99

Trust Your Instincts, Be Yourself, and Check
With a Friend 101

A Little Testosterone Goes a Long Way 102

Stand by Your Stand 105

The Notes You Take Could Save Your Career 108

A Few Short Words About the Short B-Word 109

Take Charge of Your Financial Future. 110

Down With Up-Talk and Other Bodacious Checkpoints . . 112

When Someone Takes a Stand With You 114

Culture Shock 116

5 **BODACIOUS WOMEN THRIVE ON SHIFT AND CHANGE**. 117

Change Is Inevitable; Growth Is Optional. 119

The Bodacious Leadership Big Six 121

Launch the Change Reaction 125

The Choice Is Always Yours 134

The Bodacious Thrive-on-Change Six-Pack. 137

How to Survive a Layoff 137

How to Interview in the Now Economy 141

How to Evaluate Multiple Job Offers 144

There's Almost Always More Money: What Most
Employers Don't Want You to Know When They
Talk Salary. 147

Stock Options: Explain That Again, Please 149

So You've Got the Job. Now What?. 152

6 **ONE THING I WISH I'D UNDERSTOOD BEFORE I QUIT AOL**. . . 157

Office Politics Isn't Always Pretty, but Snow White and
Sleeping Beauty Are 159

Politics Is Our Friend 162

How to Tell Whether Someone's Playing Power Games
With You 165

(Office) Size Still Matters 166

Strategies From the Political Masters 168

The Art of Quitting Well. 179

Voodoo Politics 181

7 **BREAKING THROUGH TO BODACIOUSNESS**. 183

The Choices You Make and Actions You Take Will Be
Based on Strategy, Not Survival 185

You Are More Aware of What's Happening in You
and Around You, and You Use This Information
Constructively. 186

You Are More Relaxed and More Comfortable With
Yourself and Feel Less Defensive 187

You Go From Survivor to Victor. 188

You Give Yourself More Credit. 189

You Do What It Takes to Create Your Best Physical,
Emotional, and Mental Health 191

You Are Constantly Learning 192

You Are More Effective in Achieving Your Dreams. 192

You Will Gain New Friends and Lose Others. 193

You Will Take More Risks. 194

You Will Help Other People Make Their Dreams
Come True 195

You Will Break the Rules 196

You Will Tell People What You Want. 196

You Will Control Yourself, Influence Others, and
Let the Rest Unfold 197

8 BRING IT ON! 199

What We Can Learn From New Economy Business
Mistakes 204

Your Big, Bodacious Personal Business Plan 208

Eleven Ways to Make Your Own Luck. 217

Achieving the Bodacious Goal: Like No One You've
Ever Seen Before. 230

EPILOGUE: LIFE'S SHORT, LEARN FAST 231

Bodacious Ways. 233

Recommended Reading. 235

Index 237

About the Authors. 241

Preface

Not too long ago, one of the major weekly newsmagazines ran a screaming yellow cover headline that read something like: "Everybody's Getting Rich But Me!" The implication was that by the time most of us mere mortals had noticed this magazine among the copies of *National Enquirer, Better Homes & Gardens,* and *People* . . . Oops! Another destiny boat had come and gone. In the New Economy, sister, you snooze, you lose.

And now, darn it, the New Economy is dead, the NASDAQ is on a roller coaster, and all the goodies are gone . . . .

Wait a minute. *Not true!* It's only the *myth* of the New Economy that has evaporated. The *potential* of the New Economy still thrives, and this is a perfect time for you to cash in on all the lessons we've learned in the last year or so. But you might have to change your ways just a bit. Above all, it's time to leave the "good girl" behind. The new New Economy—the Now Economy as I call it—will reward the gutsy, the bold, the audacious, the tenacious, the savvy, the adventurous. Now is the time to get *bodacious!*

In my 10 years at AOL (that's how long my dot-com "overnight success" took me) I discovered that all those characteristics of AOL that made it the huge success story it is today were the *same* qualities I needed to achieve my own full potential. Now I want to share what I learned from my personal journey in hopes of helping other women make their personal and work lives bodaciously successful—regardless of the external circumstances.

I predict that someday history will look back on the "New Economy" as the time when real, lasting success came to both men and women who knew their value, knew their purpose, and who held on tight during the wild ride that's still ahead of us. This book will show you how to do just that.

In this book I'll give you:

* Fourteen bodacious, easy internal shifts you can make to claim the self-esteem, independence, career success, and personal power you know in your heart that you deserve

* Six secrets to thriving in the New Economy—no matter *how* Wall Street is doing

* Strategies for marketing yourself bodaciously inside your company

* Your own bodacious personal business plan to set your dreams in motion

* Bodacious ways to make every change in your life a change for the *better*

You can make more money, have more fun, and achieve your dreams in the New Economy. And there's still time to do it!
I'll show you how.

Acknowledgments

Mary: It took a lot of people over a long time to affect my life in myriad ways to make this book possible. So I could say thanks to everyone I've known. However, I need to single out some who had notable impact.

First, thanks to all the AOLers past and present who made my work experience so rich, purposeful, and fun. In particular, thanks to Steve Case, Jean Case, Keith Jenkins, Mike Connors, Brian Burnett, Wendy Garcia, Norm Wilhelm, Robin Sparks, Kathy Riley, Bill Fitzgerald, and Mark Stavish. Though not an AOLer but one I consider part of my AOL experience, thanks to SARK for writing bodacious and succulent books, including *The Bodacious Book of Succulence*, that have inspired women everywhere to have the courage and spirit to venture into their most colorful, confident, and joyful expressions of themselves.

Second, thanks to my family and friends, whose support and encouragement sustained me more than I can describe or repay. Thanks to Mom and Dad for always loving me even when I broke your heart. To my siblings, Leslie, Amy, and Charley, thanks for being proud of my success. To Ruth Hill, Suzanne Martinez, Elizabeth Faulkner, Jana Bridgman, and Michael and Diana Schick, thanks for your love and support of my high times and low. Thanks to friends who broadened my professional world and believed in my abilities: Mary Saily, Burgess Levin, Kevin Karaffa, Jim Atwood, Ray Snyder, Ken Blanchard, Laura Georgantos, Patricia Cooper, Deborah Young-Kroeger, Cindy Morgan, Chris Worley, David Hitchin, Tony Petrella, and Peter Block. Special thanks to Marta Brooks, who first encouraged me years ago to capture my AOL experiences as "Wee Wee with the Big Dogs." And, finally, special thanks to Hank, the most bodacious man I know and love, for believing in my BSPB abilities long before I did.

Thanks to Ellen Kadin, Irene Majuk, Jim Bessent, and Kama Timbrell at AMACOM for immediately being enthusiastic about this project and for making my first experience with the publishing world so enjoyable. And special, special thanks to Martha Finney, whose excitement, active participation, and talent have enabled me to fulfill a dream of sharing my story with women everywhere.

Martha: I would like to thank Loyola Sylvan, Judi Neal, Lil Maland, George-Anne Fay, Nancy Croft Baker, and Melanie (Miel) Keveles for introducing me to new frontiers of gratitude. To my bodacious young nieces—Eleanore Victoria, Adria Sophia, and Morgana Rhys—learn these lessons well.

And to Mary, an eternal thanks for sharing with me a new way of looking at life and myself.

Mary and Martha: We would both like to thank the very bodacious Tiane Mitchell-Gordon. Without her, none of this would have happened.

"This above all: To thine own self be true."

"We must manage continued hypergrowth, position ourselves in an increasing complex and competitive marketplace, while simultaneously expanding into new areas."

"Any measure of success must include a sense of comfort with yourself. When you are at ease with yourself, you are able to utilize all your gifts and fulfill your purpose in life."

BODACIOUS

1

Like Nothing You've Ever Seen Before

"Life's Short, Learn Fast"

I WAS wearing those words of wisdom on my T-shirt the day I went to work without my pants.* I showed up that day as I always did, prepared to work out in America Online's luxuriously equipped fitness center before the day began, wearing my workout clothes and carrying my office clothes in my gym bag, to change into after my shower. After my shower. That was when I made the discovery: no pants. And I had an appointment with colleagues in the human

---

* This T-shirt was produced by the bodacious company Strategic Interactions (www.strategicinteractions.com), which does some very cool work and whose name echoes a major learning experience for me at AOL.

resources department in less than an hour, and then another one after that. I had no time to go home and change.

Well, that's that, I thought. I'll just have to spend the morning's back-to-back meetings in my form-fitting workout shorts and T-shirt. You know those dreams where you show up completely inappropriately dressed? I was living one. "Taking our casual dress code a little too seriously, aren't we, Mary?" was one of the many comments I suffered through that morning.

In this high-tech sea of relaxed-fitting chinos, my skin-tight Lycra shorts were transmitting data I would have preferred to keep to myself. Fortunately, the T-shirt was just long enough to cover the rear view. And its words followed me around all morning: Life is short, learn fast. Life is short, learn fast. Life is short, learn fast. You don't normally expect to get revolutionary messages from an old T-shirt you grab from a drawer in a morning so busy that you forget the rest of your clothes. But this one struck me right between the eyes.

It began a new line of information input that just wouldn't give up over the next several weeks, like those electronic news headlines that crawl around buildings in Times Square and Rockefeller Center for all the world to see. Only this one was going on in my head for only me to see:

> I'm burning out. I'm forgetting my clothes. I'm losing sleep. I'm easily distracted. This last training rollout has been all-consuming. I lost a promotion opportunity (and my lovely, private office with a view of the lake) to a man hired from the outside. Something has to give. Something has to change. Life is indeed short. I'd better listen up. I'd better learn fast.

I had been with AOL for 10 years, helping it drive one of the most historic, explosive business and economic periods of growth in history. And now it was time for me to go. It meant that I would be walking away from thousands of dollars in stock options. But to stay would mean an outcome even more unthinkable.

I would depart as AOL's first corporate training manager. I had helped AOL define the characteristics and skills it needed from its management to achieve its unparalleled stature in world corporate affairs and, more importantly, the daily lives of millions of members. The company was my home, its employees were like family, it was where I grew up. It was where I discovered what it means to be a key player in a project that would truly change the world, a project that had meaning. AOL was my professional family of origin.

But as with any family of origin, to grow you have to go. And so I resigned.

Resigning wasn't the first bodacious thing I did in my young life as a New Economy player, and it wouldn't be the last bodacious thing I did, either. But it was the moment that I saw bodaciousness for what it is: the key to thriving as the New Economy comes to a close and to prevailing as the *Now* Economy blows in and challenges us all to be even bigger, bolder, and better and to have the courage, the inner strength, to be more authentic versions of the selves we know we can be.

I learned what it means to be bodacious from the most bodacious startup of this high-tech era. But to reach my next level of success and authenticity, I had to find my future elsewhere.

"Some Computer Company"

AOL and I are both unrecognizable from the versions we were when we first met 13 years ago. Our paths crossed at similar stages in our lives. We were both young adults with some achievement on our records already. I had an engineering degree from Virginia Tech, but I had already decided I didn't want to use it. While I was in school, AOL was operating as Quantum Computer Services, providing very limited online services to a small group of Commodore 64 computer owners: games, chatrooms, e-mail, bulletin boards, that sort of thing. But management already knew that those days were numbered. We were both poised for radical change (although I'm pretty certain that Steve Case had a better idea where the company was going than I had about my own future). For both of us, what had happened in our immediate pasts was nothing like what was in store. We were both in for the ride of our lives.

We were in the same boat in other ways, too. We both started out hoping that what we were building eventually would be considered valuable by the world. We both started out sharing space with others: AOL (I mean Quantum Computer Services) shared its building with a defense consulting company (which was making far more money in those days than we were). I shared my first home with four other women, all of us finding our way in the Big City of greater Washington, DC. We both learned (Steve a lot quicker than I) to pay no attention to the criticisms and threats from antagonists who pretended to be supportive but who eventually revealed their true objective: to dominate us through fear and devaluation. We would both change our names. Only I would change my name back again.

We would both learn what it means to succeed, transforming ourselves beyond anyone's wildest imaginings. AOL would emerge as the world's largest Internet service provider and owner of HBO, CNN, *Time* magazine, and even Looney Tunes, among the vast number of businesses it absorbed by merging with Time Warner. And a decade after taking an eight-dollar-an-hour customer service representative position, I would emerge from the experience a multimillionaire with the power to invest in other companies and help other entrepreneurs make their own visions come true. But most important, I would gain both the power and the desire to help other women fulfill their destiny by giving them the encouragement and information they need to express their authenticity and drive.

But my first ambitions were decidedly more immediate and self-focused. A freshly hatched college grad in 1988, I drove up to Northern Virginia from my parents' house in Williamsburg, in their Ford Taurus, which they insisted on because they didn't trust my used Escort to have the necessary pep to keep me alive on the notorious Capital Beltway. I already had a possible room lined up in a group house. All I needed was a job to help me get up to the area. Any job would do, as long as it helped me pay my bills, make my rent, and buy me time to look around for something better. All I knew was that I didn't want to turn my hard-won degree into an engineering career (much to the dismay of my parents). I could have started making the big bucks right away if I had stuck with engineering. I had no idea what I wanted—not exactly the mark of an educated young woman destined for greatness. Pretty darned pitiful, by all external measures. All I can say is that I was headed for sheer dumb luck, navigated only by my intuition.

And I was glad to be heading north to the city. Over the weeks immediately after my graduation, my mother had become increasingly antsy about my finding work—or rather my *not* finding work. Life in Williamsburg didn't hold much promise for a new grad unless I wanted to put on a farthingale and guide people around colonial mansions in the historic district, or button up a dirndl and help Busch Garden visitors pretend that they were in the Old Country. I knew I needed to go to a big metropolitan area to discover what I didn't even know to look for yet.

And so it was in the *Washington Post* that I saw the ad for customer service representatives for a computer company. It looked moderately tolerable and interesting, so I called the number in the ad. And called again. And called again. No one responded to my messages. I could have interpreted that as indifference, taken it personally, and just stopped trying. But with the last try, I got through and got an appointment for an interview.

I had two interviews that swampy July day: one with a temporary help company and one with Quantum Computer Services, which placed the ad. I was dressed for success. In fact, I thought I looked pretty darned with-it: a blue and white seersucker suit, pantyhose, dark blue pumps, matching post earrings, white linen blouse, and a black vinyl portfolio I bought especially for the occasion because I thought it would make me more professional.

The ladies at the temp agency said, "Thanks, we'll call you." But even as I walked out the door, I knew they wouldn't. I was a miserable failure at every single typing, filing, dictation, and grammar test they put in front of me. A degree in industrial engineering does not prepare you to be office help, I discovered.

But Cindy at Quantum said, "Can you start July 11th?" And with that question, I took my place among the ranks of only a few people who were pouring the foundations for what eventually became known as the New Economy.

At eight dollars an hour and at the lowest possible rank in the company, I figured, "Good, I have a job. Now I can get started in *something*."

My parents told their friends, "Our daughter works in customer service for some computer company."

Where the Boys Are

As one of the few women in the country entering the workforce with a high-tech company (however lowly my job was) and as a daughter of the so-called postfeminist era, I didn't give much thought to women's workplace issues. Even the fact that the call center management was informally known as the All Men's Club didn't bother me. I was just glad to be in this adrenaline-charged environment where so much creativity, vision, and innovation were harnessed into this thing called online services. I saw nothing to criticize about the way women were treated in my early years with AOL. There were women in powerful leadership roles from the beginning, so I knew I had upward mobility. I was just glad to be part of this really cool mission! I rose quickly through the ranks, with rapid raises and promotions. I was given the chance time and again to take on responsibilities that were completely new to me. With a few exceptions (which I'll talk about later in the book) I felt treated fairly and acknowledged regularly for my contributions.

But because I still had such a long way to go before I scraped the glass ceiling, it didn't register with me that year after year after year, the highest executive ranks held (and as of this writing, continue to hold) hardly any women at all. My gifts for being upbeat, effective, good at communication, good at building teams, and creating valuable products for helping others succeed were all commonly associated with female roles. I was rewarded well for helping others. But after 10 years, my career at AOL came to a dead stop with one word: *strategic*. I wasn't strategic enough, I was told by my boss, who otherwise often told me how indispensable I was.

This criticism never came up in my performance appraisals. Becoming more strategic was never factored into any career management plan or objectives that my boss and I had agreed upon. And with that one word, gone was my next best hope for a promotion within the department that I cared so deeply about. Gone was my lovely office, which I had to relinquish to the man who was hired from the outside for that position. And gone was my faith that my future was in AOL.

I wasn't "ready," my boss said, to take on the role of director. But I suspect that it was my boss who wasn't ready to perceive me with the formal title officially acknowledging the responsibilities I was already shouldering. And this was *before* the no-pants episode. In truth, I was being more strategic than he would ever know. Over the years I was helping AOL pump knowledge, motivation, and leadership skills into thousands of its employees as it became more and more a major player in everyday America, I was strategically surviving a marriage that made me feel controlled and afraid. Within a few months of our little "strategy" conversation, I strategically designed a way to safely leave my husband for the second and final time—a plan that involved a waiting friend, a joint meeting with our therapist, who would witness and temper any reaction he might have, and my car already completely packed with my necessary belongings. You want strategy? I was strategy personified.

I was *bodaciousness* personified. I had come a long way, I had left a lot behind me, and now it seemed that my last departure would be the company I had invested so many years and so much passion in. And I had joined the ranks of statistics, this time the statistics of ambitious American women whose value to their corporations is lost and whose careers risk being derailed by the failure (either their employers' or their own) to accurately capture the true value of their contributions and potential.

With all this talk about America's new wealth and the opportunity that's available for anyone with a great résumé or a cool business plan, many women are still not players. The promise of what was once the New Economy has benefited women, to be sure. We are so much better off than we were 30 years ago. But we still have a long way to go. And with the New Economy behind us, now having entered a phase that I'm calling the Now Economy, we have to seize the opportunities and claim even more of our share of the benefits of market demand and economic opportunity. These opportunities depend on the present, the now. *Now* is always relevant to your career and economic success. *Now* is always changing. And *now* is the best time to get started reengineering our approach to our careers and the real power women have to make a significant difference in the corporate marketplace and to enjoy the rewards of doing so.

Here is a fact of the Now Economy: Women are so sought-after in the high-tech job market that headhunters have been known to pay their spies and sources $120 for each professional female name and her job description in Silicon Valley, where they may only pay $80 for a man's name. You would think that we'd take advantage of that demand and insist on salaries that are equal to a man's. But we don't. Throughout all industry sectors women are still making only three-quarters what men make for comparable jobs. In the information technology (IT) sector alone—a sector that's supposed to be so modern, so progressive, so egalitarian, *so* needy for talent— women make just 85 percent of what men are making. So somewhere between the headhunting stage and the job offer, we've allowed 15 percent of our value in the marketplace to evaporate.

How can that be? Discrimination laws are in place to fight pay inequities. We have plenty of how-to books giving us the skill sets of negotiating, playing office politics, and "winning at the boys' game," which is basically the message: You must overcome the fact that you're female every single day. And books on work/life balance, still written primarily for women, continue to put on our shoulders the responsibility of how much of ourselves we're willing to trade away for the sake of career, romantic love, dependent children, or aging parents.

In the meantime, how are women being treated as viable players in the economy? Like outsiders who are invited to play only if we can somehow find a way to fit in. Yes, there are indeed women entrepreneurs in the high-tech and dot.com sectors. As of this writing, Carly Fiorina is still in charge of Hewlett-Packard. But we know this only because it's so extraordinary that the media have pointed it out to us: "See? Look, there *are* skirts in the executive suite." Excellent groups, such as Girlgeeks.com and Women in Technology, Inc. (www.witi.org), are dedicated to encouraging the participation of women in high-tech sectors where the big paychecks and the big opportunities reside. Wouldn't it be nice if we didn't need them anymore?

But we do need those organizations because the old New Economy marketplace is still not in the habit of remembering that we're part of the scene too. For example, the April 2000 issue of *Business 2.0*, the respected magazine reporting on and serving New Economy businesses, featured the following mix of men and women among its advertisements: There are eighty-five images of men as decisionmakers, compared with only eleven images of women as decisionmakers (and one of them appears in a scenario in which she inherited an Old Economy business from Daddy). There are even two ads in which women are depicted as the manifestation of the buying decision you don't want to make. (There are also six infants, two dogs, one cat, one duck, one very weird psychic [female, but still weird], one exploding volcano, and one belly button [most definitely that of a woman—or a guy who could use some serious crunches].)

And that's the present. The future needs some remedial intervention as well. In its 2000 study, *Tech-Savvy: Educating Girls in the New Computer Age*, the American Association of University Women reported that

* Girls represent 17 percent of the computer science advanced-placement (AP) test takers and less than 10 percent of the higher-level computer science AP test takers.

* Women are roughly 20 percent of IT professionals.

* Women receive less than 28 percent of the computer science bachelor's degrees, down from a high of 37 percent in 1984. Computer science is the only field in which women's participation has decreased over time.

* Women make up just 9 percent of the recipients of engineering-related bachelor's degrees.

I'm not saying that high-tech or IT careers are the only avenues to Now Economy success, but I would like to see evidence of more women considering these high-reward fields. The environment is not actively hostile to women. Of course, there are male decision-makers in power that just can't wrap their brains around the notion of women being leaders and participants in powerful organizations, especially high-tech ones. But for the most part, I'd say it's more a *neglectful* environment, rolling like that big ball in the Indiana Jones movie down a track that it started on with no particular thought about the presence and participation of women in these high-reward careers.

Is this something to get furious about? Well, you can if you want to. But that's wasting precious time and energy. Don't get mad, get effective. Get *bodacious!*

We will finally achieve our bodaciousness tipping point when *Fortune* magazine publishes its last annual list of Top Women in Business and we all ask, "So what?" I'm sure that most of the women on this year's list have done so already. Let's join them, shall we?

"Better I Should Suffer"

In a way, it would be better if we were dealing with an openly hostile environment because it's easier to see and it's just plain illegal. And we could fight that. But we are surrounded by well-meaning men and women who sincerely respect us but truly don't see women in the role of director or higher, as strategic players in the chase for commercial competitiveness, or in any other position of power, for that matter. Men and women both have been culturally encoded to look elsewhere for power and profitable effectiveness on the corporate scene. And we've been culturally encoded to set aside our personal power, the drive, energy, and fire of our fullest authenticity, in the name of being nice, being good girls, being accommodating, and permitting the neglectful (not necessarily purposeful) devaluation of our contributions because speaking up for ourselves would be *confrontational!* Which starts with C, which rhymes with B, which stands for—well, not *bodacious.* We're sent messages every day that this is really a man's world, an All Men's Club, and that we may be allowed to participate only if we mind our manners. Yes, we've made huge strides and achievements, but still many of us feel as though we're living a Ladies' Night at an exclusive men's club, a special dispensation that might continue as long as the members find it expedient and amusing.

We don't all feel this way all the time, but most of us feel that extra pressure every now and then. And in the process, we're made to feel suspicious about each other. I think almost all of us have heard someone say, "No one's harder on women in business than women." I haven't seen any statistic supporting that, have you? But I also haven't heard anyone speak up and say, "What a crock!" Well, here's my vote.

Let's take a look at some of the commercials that reflect what our culture considers acceptable:

* A little girl no older than ten talks confidently to adults about how she takes care of her big brother's hankering for a fruit drink. I would like to suggest the bodacious alternative: "Sure you can have some, Billy. Packets are in the cupboard, pitcher's on the shelf, spoon's in the drawer, water's in the faucet. Knock yourself out."

* A secretary (we assume) is on the phone with Big Boss ("Sir"), reporting that the staff, one by one, is out: late, having a haircut, going to kick-boxing, and so on. The boss says, "Isn't there anyone there who knows how much business can be done before 8 A.M.?" "Sure," she says, and

hands the receiver to an *outsider*, the UPS man. The bodacious alternative: "Sure. And you're talking to her. I'd like
to talk to you about my taking on added responsibility."

* At a business reception, Wife of Clearly Clueless Doofus
meets his gorgeous and appropriately dressed assistant.
There is talk about the two of them traveling together.
Subtitles reveal wife's obsession with assistant's flat stomach
and "logically" concluded assumptions that her husband's
about to get poached by Gorgeous Assistant. (How many
different things can you find wrong with this commercial?)
The bodacious alternative: "I'm so glad to meet you. I'm
sure we'll be good friends. And (in a whispered aside) say,
I'd love the name of your personal trainer."

* A businesswoman hollers out, "That's my cab!" just as a
businessman reaches for the car door handle. Good for her!
But then in a higher, appeasing voice she asks, "Share the
cab with me?" His response: "Sure, why not!" like he's doing
her some kind of a favor. The bodacious alternative: "If
we're going the same way, you're welcome to share the cab
with me." Notice the statement form and the condition to
the offer. And the Bodacious Man would respond, "That's
very generous of you, I'd appreciate it."

Why make such a big deal about such trivial things as commercials? Am I saying that the women of the twenty-first century are
being dominated by diabolical advertisers who conspire against us
in walnut-paneled offices high above Madison Avenue? No, of
course not. But what is significant about these examples is that they
are the product of some of the best creative minds in the country,
they've been exhaustively run by focus groups of ordinary citizens
who have passed their approval on them. And evidently no one
thought there was anything wrong with them!

We all know better than to interpret any kind of commercial as
the gospel truth. But they must ring true on some visceral level to

effectively convert the viewers into buyers. And this is where these commercials reflect the deep-seated, culturally encoded assumptions of how women are expected to behave, especially in the context of our relationships with others: "We should put the needs of others before our own." "We should suspect other women." "We should expect that others will suspect *us*." "If our boss undervalues our work, then we must assume that our work has no value." "We must value care and nurturing over anything else, even it means getting into a car with a stranger."

And what it all boils down to is this one simple message: Be perfect. Be a good girl. Be nice. Don't offend. Do whatever you need to do to keep relationships intact. Because it can all fall apart around you with one slip of selfishness. And then you'll be left with nothing but the blame you so richly deserve.

For most American women, the burden is in the accumulated nicks and cuts in our careers and private lives. An acquaintance asks us for an outrageous and imposing favor and we can't say "no." We discover that our paycheck isn't as much as our male counterparts', and we blame ourselves for not being better negotiators. We're not included in an important social occasion with our male colleagues and customers. Our pleasure-reading magazines focus on work and family balance, recipes, lovemaking techniques, and beauty tips. Our mate's magazines (the ones he lets us see) focus on adventure travel, car stereos, nature stories, and modern electronics.

So in a high-tech era that thrives on shift and change and extraordinary wealth, we still experience Old Economy feelings. How many of these can you relate to:

* The feeling of being out of control of your time? Your day? Your priorities?

* The feeling of suspecting other people's motives?

* The feeling of being overwhelmed?

* The feeling that somehow you missed the boat of life-changing opportunity?

* The feeling that you're falling behind the times?

* The feeling that you're not living up to your potential?

* The feeling that you've been victimized or at least taken advantage of?

* The feeling that you're being left out?

* The feeling that you're about to lose your job through organizational change rather than through any fault of your own?

These are very real and valid feelings of women today, based on old behaviors and social coding that has no place in our society anymore. Because of the demands and opportunities that have been made available to most of us in the Now Economy, we are under increasing pressure to give the world what it has never seen before.

Start-up companies tend to think of that mandate as offering revolutionary products and services. But we're all start-ups in today's economic environment. That means that we're all responsible for delivering to the world what it has never seen before. And that means you!

We're All Start-Ups

As AOL and I grew up together, I discovered that new companies and Now Economy people—men and women both—have a lot in common. We are all start-ups. Resting on who we were even yesterday puts us in danger of being overrun, being supplanted, and becoming obsolete. The future is hard to predict, but we plan as wisely as we can, always watching for what emerges and doing our best to be prepared to respond. In the Now Economy, one change of circumstances or course of events, even a seemingly small or isolated one, can have a huge effect and cause us all to redefine ourselves once again. But regardless of our circumstances, the goal remains the same: to be relevant and effective so we can not only survive but also thrive, reaching our greatest potential.

Both companies and people can stay fresh, energized, and competitive by the constant renewal of the start-up phase. An economy driven by technological innovation demands it. Likewise, as Now Economy people we're going to be under even more pressure to prove that we can deliver innovation and return on investment. It's not enough anymore to be slick and trendy, hooked up with a cutting-edge company that's doing "way cool" things. We have to concretely show how our contributions add to corporate earnings. And in our private lives, we're under increasing pressure to demonstrate to our most powerful stockholder (ourselves) that our business plan (our life) continues to be valid, continues to be relevant, and continues to be worth the time, energy, devotion, and emotion we invest in it every day. My guess is that this newly accelerated interest in personal effectiveness is what has caused the explosion of personal coaches as celebrities these days. (If this book has found its way into your hands, I bet you've at least heard of Laura Berman Fortgang and Cheryl Richardson.)

Not only have coaches found their way into our hearts to help us break out onto new levels of potential, but so have entrepreneurs. They've taken on a new sheen of celebrity that we haven't seen since the likes of the Vanderbilts, Carnegies, and Rockefellers. But that can be very misleading. Reading the memoirs of Bill Gates, Michael Dell, or Andy Grove is great, but not enough, unless you want to launch your own Microsoft, Dell Computers, or Intel. Maybe you don't have the drive to take computers apart and build them back up again in your garage or basement. Maybe the word *mogul* and the "your picture here" silhouette just never seemed right together. Maybe leadership on such a gladiator scale just doesn't interest you. It's just not real life to most people in this universe.

However, bodaciousness is within our reach (and it should be), no matter who we are.

To be a bodacious Now Economy player, we'd all do better to take our lessons and inspirations from the Now Economy companies themselves and from the stories of the thousands of ordinary civilians, like me, who huffed and puffed and breathed life into these amazing life-changing, world-rearranging organizations. We had to embody and be prepared to do battle as start-ups ourselves before we could expect to bring little Quantum Computer Services forward and launch it into the stratosphere as AOL, with its more than 29 million members, more than 71 million pieces of daily e-mail, and its megalithic media impact.

You may be a fan of AOL or you may detest it, but there's no denying the impact it has had on U.S. culture and the way Americans spend their time. Taking a small company serving mostly techno-geeks, professors, and Defense Department nerds and transforming it into a national living room where Grandpa can sit at his computer and watch a video clip of Billy sing "Little Bunny Foo Foo" took a lot of long hours, a lot of vision, a lot of spine, and massive boda-ciousness from all AOL employees. We were all bodacious start-ups!

To thrive in the Now Economy, start-up individuals must be:

EVOLUTIONARY. Most people don't realize that AOL's first online service wasn't for PCs or even Macs. It was for the Commodore 64 computer, the best-selling home computer in the mid-1980s. This machine carried the first iteration of Steve Case's vision for a graphically based online service known as Q-Link. And from that first version to today's AOL service, it's been a constant evolution of improving the member's experience. In our private lives we're consistently building on what has come before, whether it's increasing our know-how or expanding our "service" to preexisting communities of clients (whether they are our parents, mates, children, or mailing lists of preferred customers). When we're in despair or feel as though we have to correct what seems a major misstep in our lives, we're tempted to throw away all that's come before, good or bad, and start from square one. That perspective makes it so much harder on us. We always have something of value to start with. It's bodacious to give ourselves credit where it's due and build on what we've got.

PIONEERING. Eventually it's not enough to pour wine from old skins into new bottles. Completely new vineyards must be sown. Completely new varieties of grapes must be cultivated. And you have to break entirely new ground to do it. Thanks to Steve Case's vision of what was possible as an online experience, whole new populations were introduced to computers and the fun and practical advantages of tapping into cyberspace. It wasn't just innovation that expanded our membership base from a few thousand computer geeks to millions of regular folks who want to send baby pictures with the click of a button. It was pioneering.

As bodacious start-up individuals we must also be pioneering. It might mean changing careers five times. It might mean ending a relationship. It might mean being the first in the family to go to college. Or being the first to start a business. Or the first to say "no" to a family heritage of alcoholism. Pioneering is breaking completely new ground. Being willing to risk failure, certainly. And maybe even failing (at least at your perceived objective). But that doesn't make you any less bodacious. In fact, being willing to continue to pioneer after setbacks is ultra-bodacious.

NIMBLE. To pioneer and allow evolution to take place in our careers and personal lives we must be nimble and flexible. As a trainer and then call center manager, I used to tell new customer service reps that if they didn't like change that would demand constant adjustment on their part, they were going to hate working at AOL. But if they preferred things to keep moving and not get boring, they'd come to the right place. As a company, AOL was continually reviewing its strategy and modifying its tactics in the marketplace, and they needed employees who could operate the same way.

Being nimble may never get boring, but that doesn't mean that it's never painful or frustrating. During my years at AOL I found myself suddenly working for someone different because of a reorganization, after I'd spent time and effort developing a good rapport with my boss. Friends were laid off. Other times a project that I cared about ended abruptly. It helps tremendously not to take changes personally. Survey the surroundings, dust yourself off, and keep moving.

TENACIOUS. The road to greatness is a rocky ride. The better you are at what you do, the more ambitious your dreams are, the rockier that ride is likely to be. And the more interested certain factions will be in the rise and (perhaps) demise of your dreams. No matter what your dream is, if it's big enough, there will be times when the only way you can achieve it is to grip the sides of your rocky little boat with all the tenacity you can muster. The biggest test of our tenacity at AOL came during what I call the connectivity crisis of 1996–1997. All our competitors had gone to flat rate pricing, but we were still charging by the minute for online time. To be competitive we knew we had to join the competition and make our service equally affordable, so we did the market predictions. We did the financial projections. We estimated what kind of load it would put on the system. We did all the due diligence possible. We flipped the switch to flat rate pricing, and FOOM!, the system was almost instantaneously overloaded. We were swamped with new members, and everyone wanted to sign on and stay signed on, leaving no room for anyone else to squeeze their way in. Within six weeks thirty-seven state attorneys general were suing us.

But we hung in there, week after week, month after month, adding new modems, new access numbers, greater capacity. Our competitors and other detractors predicted that we'd implode under the weight of our rapid growth. But we didn't. They predicted that we'd lose a critical mass of original members. But we didn't. As a team we resolved, "This isn't going to kill us." And it didn't. We hung in there.

The price was long hours for some, sleepless nights for some, time away from our families and friends. Six months later: Oh, the party we had! The reward was millions of new members, millions of satisfied and reassured existing members, and fresh respect from everyone: the members, Wall Street, individual investors, the press, family, friends, ourselves, and each other.

LONELY. There will be people whose opinions you care about who just won't get you. People often see you only for who you are now, not for the vision you're holding for your future self. Only a handful of people truly understood what Steve Case and his small band of visionaries really had in mind—those who could put their money where their imaginations were.

Think of the satisfaction you'll have when you prove the naysayers wrong. (Revenge, by the way, is not bodacious. But the satisfaction of being right in the midst of discouragement is definitely bodacious.)

Somebody's Going to Want a Piece of You

You've heard the stories of lottery winners suddenly discovering family members they never knew they had. You know the expression, "Nothing succeeds like success." Both of those scenarios are true for bodacious start-ups. As you become successful in turning your unique gifts and vision into a successful career, some people will want to borrow or steal your resources. Maybe it's a client list, or an introduction, or a proprietary approach to solving a business problem. Maybe it's your time and emotional energy as a friend perceives you as stronger than she is and wants to spend hour upon hour rehashing a personal problem, seeking your guidance, and then responding to each suggestion with "Yes, but. . . ."

I'm not suggesting that you routinely turn down all requests for favors (that's not bodacious, either). Just be prepared: The greater your level of achievement and success, the more you will be asked to grant or deny requests; therefore the more vigilant you must be in protecting your assets (even intangible assets, such as time) from being pilfered right under your nose.

Drawing boundaries is a bodacious challenge for women who were brought up to believe that saying "no," that choosing not to share, was simply not nice. Nice is not the issue here. Respecting your own boundaries (where *you* choose to draw them) is good for your community of friends, family, and clients, too. Protect your assets. They're your gift to your world. If you're sucked dry, you're good for no one.

This Is High-Wire Living

If you're feeling a sense of greater risk and peril, you're right. The more you reach for, the more you stand to gain. Unfortunately, you have more to lose. Rather, *fortunately*, you have more to lose. The name of the game is to have more: more confidence, more joie de vivre, more enjoyable ways to express your authenticity, and, of course, more financial security.

But greater losses lie in never having taken the gamble in the first place. Consider the New Testament story (Matthew 25: 14-30) of the master and servants and the talents. The master was leaving for a long trip, so he decided to entrust a few of his servants with his property while he was gone. He gave one guy five talents (originally a large amount of money, now symbolic of abilities), one guy two talents, and the last guy just one talent. The first two servants went out and used their money to make more money, which involved some risk, I'm sure. Each doubled his lot. The last guy was so scared of losing the single talent that he buried it until the owner came home. Upon homecoming, the master was thrilled with the two servants who successfully doubled the money and gave them great big rewards. However, he was infuriated with the servant who took no chances with what he had. Staying on par wasn't good enough; the master expected growth and development. Then, talk about a pink slip. The guy was told that he was worthless and was thrown out into the "darkness, where there will be weeping and gnashing of teeth." Ouch! I don't think the master was a particularly nasty guy. He just thought that not proactively using what you have was a crime and that being scared was no excuse. The two other servants had their share of shaking in their boots but took action anyway. The master and his two remaining servants would kick butt in today's Now Economy.

Why "Now"?

The New Economy was exciting while it lasted, and it made thousands of ordinary Americans very rich. And for those of us it was very good to, it would have been very nice if it had endured a little while longer. But I expect that we'll come to regard the New Economy as merely a transitionary period between the Old Economy (that is, every market condition that existed before the introduction of the commercial possibilities of the Internet, other amazing technology, and globalization) and the long stretch ahead of us that I call the Now Economy.

The reason why the New Economy lasted only five years (some say from August 1995, when Netscape went public, to April 2000, when NASDAQ had its first major disillusioning meltdown) was that it fell victim to its own hatchet: the demand for instant reward and immediate and ongoing gratification. In his book *New Rules for the New Economy*, author Kevin Kelly wrote, "It's a 'hits' economy, where resources flow to those that show some life. If a new novel, new product, or new service begins to succeed, it is fed more; if it falters, it's left to wither. Them that has, gets more."

Everything was fast, dynamic, aggressive, and adrenaline-pushed. Straight up seemed to be the only way to go—never mind the grossly overvalued companies, stock prices, and hopes. But as soon as it lost its own promise of being a sustainable hit, BOOM! All done! Investors pulled out. High-demand employees were laid off. Talking heads on television tried to make us think they could see it coming a mile away.

Naysayers predict that the chartline will plummet and we'll dive into an economic Dark Ages. But I don't think that will happen. I think we'll continue an overall upward climb. But instead of it being a steep climb high into the stratosphere, I predict it will be more like a helix. 'Round and 'round we'll go, gently attaining new levels of prosperity in smaller steps, with the chance to enjoy the view as we ascend. The Now Economy will put new challenges at our feet, asking us to integrate our new selves (the high-tech, high-potential, high-pressure climate) with our old selves (the Old Economy environment that rewards patience and perspective).

Unlike the New Economy (which seemed to be reserved for high-tech entrepreneurs and the people lucky to work for them), the Now Economy is for everyone. No one is excused or exempt from showing up. Whether you're an engineer, an account executive, or a waitress in the donut shop, you are touched by the Now Economy. Although the Now Economy will never be completely defined, it will emphasize continuous growth, continuous achievement, continuous investment, and continuous reward. No more straight shots. But if we're lucky, there'll be no more steep plunges, either.

If you considered yourself a New Economy outsider, you haven't missed the boat with the Now Economy. The New Economy, for all its opportunity, also felt like an exclusive club for the chic geek: crazy hours, crazy money, crazy food (contiguous pizza meals), young girls dressed in black wearing fascist glasses, and everyone living and working in lofts in SoHo, Silicon Valley, Silicon Alley, Silicon Prairie, and Silicon Dominion. Kids who don't even keep their rooms straight at home owned architectural landmarks gleaming in glass and angles all over the countryside that was once orchards and cow pastures.

If you were a New Economy insider, I have two words for you: "regular hours." Whether you're an insider or an outsider, try not to pass moral judgment on the New Economy itself. It was neither good nor bad. It just was.

But the *Now* Economy—there's an opportunity!

It will be like nothing we've ever seen before. And it will be the bodacious who will enjoy the ride.

The Trip to Bodaciousness

Bodacious! Is that even a word? Yes, it's in the dictionary. And it means outstanding, bold, and audacious. Even the way you say "bodacious" can only be bodacious. Bo-DAY-shus!

It's usually considered a southern term. You can hear hillbillies saying it in your mind's ear. And then it became a frat term. Horny guys say "bodacious ta-tas," and you immediately understand what they're talking about. But it's also a great word for women to claim for themselves: It brings up a vigorous feeling of being courageous, creative, larger than life, and self-respecting, being completely, madly, thoroughly, full-speed-ahead, exactly who you are and relishing the experience, with apologies to no one.

Although I would never say that a single word changed my life (that would be silly), I can say that it became my own personal rallying cry. Three little syllables helped me change my life, and now its spirit is helping me create a new life that is leading me to an even greater sense of who I can be and what I can give the world.

When I look in the mirror, I see someone like no one I have ever seen before. I see someone who benefited from the New Economy in ways most people don't even bother to dream about.

But I also see someone who is no longer afraid. I'm not afraid anymore of my own abilities. I'm not afraid anymore of my own confidence. I'm not afraid anymore of my place in the world or what people will think of me if I step forward in full bodaciousness. I'm not afraid anymore of people thinking I'm not a good girl. I'm not afraid anymore of letting my vulnerabilities show, if and when I choose. And I'm not afraid anymore of showing my power, experience, and expertise if and when I choose.

This Is High-Performance Living

Every day Now Economy companies and Now Economy individuals must ask themselves the same questions: Who am I today? Who do I want to be tomorrow? What do I need to do, get, or learn to reach my goals? These are soul-searching questions. Yet if we don't grapple with them (and keep grappling with them as we and our environment change), the answers will be made for us, and we may not like them. If we don't play the game, we will lose it. To some extent this has always been true. The difference is that today the rate of change is accelerating the effects of our participation—or lack thereof.

The wonderful thing about the Now Economy is that it presents so much possibility if we have the courage to define who we want to be in it. This same level of possibility presents no firm ground, no firm rules, and therefore lots of opportunity for both success and failure. Our personal risk tolerance is tested and challenged over and over again.

To take that challenge again and again, you've got to be willing to walk the Bodacious Way. After the first heavy push, the going will be easier with each new challenge. But first some foundation work must be laid. You must integrate an internal shift in the way you relate to the world with new skills for thriving in the Now Economy. And this is where this book will help.

In these chapters you will learn to:

1. Look within for personal power

2. Use your relationships more strategically

3. Take a stand

4. Thrive on shift and change

5. Accept and use office politics to help you

6. Create a strategic personal business plan to become the Bodacious Woman you want to be

I also include sixteen sidebars full of practical advice on everything from surviving a layoff to landing a Now Economy job to taking charge of your financial future.

In companies, both high-tech and low, there are millions of women throughout the United States and the world wondering what their role will be. This is the time to begin capitalizing on the opportunities the Now Economy will create. My hunch is that this particular trend isn't going away anytime soon and that it will stretch into the future for at least another 15 years. You can jump in any time.

But right now would be a really good idea!

Bodaciousness Starts on the Inside

WHEN YOU live your life bodaciously, you get what you deserve: loving and respectful relationships, exciting work, promotions, raises, great projects, and irresistible job offers.* But these are only the external manifestations of the Bodacious Way. Bodacious women know that these rewards come more easily and authentically when you are bodacious within. All the skills, techniques, and political savvy in the world won't stick until we improve the quality of our inner messages and discover how the ways we speak to ourselves are actually the major factor in the way we build for

---

* This isn't to say that you don't deserve these wonderful things if you don't live bodaciously. It's just that you reduce your chances of getting them.

ourselves a fabulous life. The good news here is that the bodacious inner voice is supportive, simple, honest, and, best of all, gentle.

In her book *Simple Abundance*, Sarah Ban Breathnach wrote,

> Going within opens the eyes of your awareness in gentle ways. You start to treat yourself more kindly. As you become intimate with your authentic self and see glimmers of the woman you truly are inside, you shore up the courage to take the first tentative steps necessary to help her evolve and emerge outwardly.

These words eloquently express the process of this authentic path. The first step is looking within (often motivated by pain); the second is treating yourself more kindly and more respectfully (as you begin to identify and define your boundaries, you also notice how you might be invading your own boundaries through self-destructive or nonnurturing habits). The third is mustering courage in new ways (such as seeking out other bodacious women for support), and the last is giving outward expression to the changes that have been evolving inside. That last step will show up in a variety of ways, from taking a stand when your boundaries have been violated, to weeding out certain people from your life, to improving your career potential, to seeing more money in your paycheck, to suddenly feeling as though you have control over the way you function in the workplace and relate more powerfully to powerful colleagues.

Over the years I've heard words coming from other women's mouths (and sometimes my own) that, when reviewed closely and honestly, show there's still inner work to be done—not just from women just starting their careers but from women solidly in middle management trying to work their way into more senior positions. Managers, directors, vice presidents, general managers, still say such things as:

"I trusted them. They didn't tell me I was about to be cut out of the project."

"I got passed over for a promotion. The guy who got it was clearly less qualified."

"This person set me up."

"I was the only woman on the team, and I wasn't invited to the weekend retreat."

"I didn't want to risk alienating the boss, so I didn't express my opinion. Someone else did, though, and got a high-profile assignment as a result."

How can this still be a problem for women when we were supposed to have come so far up the success and potential ladders by now? Even former Secretary of State Madeleine Albright, with all her accomplishments and world stature, tells stories of how she still finds herself staying quiet in a meeting only to have someone else articulate (and get the credit for) precisely what she was thinking. We're into our third decade of so-called postfeminist power in organizations, but we're still dragging along some heavy mental burdens that are causing us to hold ourselves back. A sense of victimization, or *learned helplessness*, as psychiatrists put it, is one of the most insidious of them all.

Isn't your day full and complex enough without a bunch of feelings of helplessness layered on top of it? Unfortunately, at the risk of sounding sexist and drawing gross generalizations, that's what we women do. We take in data, interpret it in precisely the way that will cause us the most pain possible, and then use the results to create perceived barriers that stop us before we even know it. What a waste of energy, emotions, and confidence!

Maybe you've seen an infrared photograph of a house with bad insulation. Reds and oranges radiate from all the vulnerable spots in a home: the windows, the doors, the attic, and thin spots in the outer walls. Now imagine taking an infrared photo of the women you pass in the halls of your office. Reds and oranges radiate from them as well (and from you, too). Here's what some of these colors are called:

Frustration

Resentment

Disappointment

Confusion

Stress

Anger

Paranoia

Suspicion

Mistrust

Intimidation

Betrayal

Shame

This is an emotional audit, measuring our reactions to our lives and the way we choose to interpret and internalize our external experiences. Certainly all these emotions have merit, but if we let them drive the way we perceive ourselves in the Now Economy world, they could be leading us down an unnecessarily destructive path.

Take an infrared photo of the bodacious woman, and you will probably see some of the same colors, but those reds and oranges won't be as blazing and all-encompassing. And you'll also see the calm, cool, soothing shades of blue that reflect these emotions:

Confidence

Control

Serenity

Victory

Creative satisfaction

Courage

Hope

Assured ambition

What's the primary difference between the two? As the bodacious woman acquires the skills necessary to thrive authentically in the Now Economy, she also cultivates an inner emotional environment that will support and nourish her deep within where no external storms can rattle her windows. In other words, bodaciousness begins within. The shift in the way you let things in will create a shift in the way you perceive the outside world. This, in turn, will create a shift in the way the world perceives you. And suddenly you're no longer the victim, you're a player.

We'll get into actual bodacious skills and techniques in the following chapters, but at this point it's most important to explore the powerful inner world that bodacious women create for themselves by the ways they choose to think—about themselves, about their careers, about any situation they're facing at any given moment.

The Inside Story: Fourteen Bodacious Ways for Career and Personal Power

BODACIOUS WOMEN MAKE THEIR SELF-ESTEEM PRIORITY ONE

Self-esteem is the climate control in your life's house. No matter what is raging outside, when your self-esteem is healthy and functioning, you are safe, dry, and secure within. Unfortunately, our culture tends to confuse self-esteem with self-absorption, self-centeredness, or just plain selfishness, and we discourage women from putting themselves first. It's still seen as somehow charming to be modest to the point of self-deprecation ("this old thing?"), to be demure to the point of stepping out of our own spotlight that we worked so hard to create, to make the comfort and happiness of others the hallmark of our own success to the point of being perversely proud of our own discomfort. That's a lot of leverage to hold against our potential.

But it's not charming to siphon off our best creative energies by playing this foolish (even cowardly) game. It's insincere and inauthentic, and it takes the power from the moments when we are truly humble. How many ways do you use the expression, "I'm sorry"? When you're truly apologizing? When you want someone to repeat something? When you need to interrupt a conversation for a legitimate purpose? When you really want to put someone in his place and are hoping that he'll pick up the edge of your biting sarcasm? I'm sorry, you don't really think that works, do you?

Observe the many ways you might be putting yourself down without even knowing it. Telling jokes about yourself. Confessing feelings of inadequacy to clients, coworkers, or bosses. Taking on assignments of lesser quality or no long-term benefit. Letting peer pressure put you in the position of taking on chores, such as cleaning out the break room refrigerator, going on donut runs, or arranging office parties. Accepting a salary that is less than what was advertised. Allowing vague, unmeasurable, or unprovable criticisms go unchallenged in your performance appraisal. In fact, it's a safe bet that any moment of harbored resentment that you can name carries with it a little story of how you put your self-esteem in second place in favor of something or someone that holds no true value for you.

Putting your self-esteem first doesn't mean that you care for others any less. It means that you care for yourself more, certainly more than you have. To have healthy self-esteem doesn't mean that you spend hours gazing into a hand mirror (in fact, don't you know some women with low self-esteem who spend a lot of precious time worrying about their appearance?). It doesn't mean that you consider yourself the Queen of All That Is Perfect, so that everyone should kneel at your feet. It doesn't mean that you go around bragging (but it *does* mean that you celebrate your good news with others). It means you're accomplishing goals more freely, and that's obvious to everyone who stands and marvels, "She makes it look so easy."

It doesn't mean that you cut in line, take the largest piece, or even serve yourself first. But it does mean serving yourself well. It means knowing what you value, welcome into your life, and fully appreciate once it's there. It also means knowing what you don't welcome into your life. It means choosing friends who share your joie de vivre and avoiding acquaintances who sap your energy (so they don't get closer and eventually tap into your values of loyalty). It means choosing organizations that reflect your most positive beliefs and values, and it means staying away from those that don't. It means loving the body you have, accepting all forms of pleasure as part of your birthright, and joyfully seeking out the people and activities that remind you of how wonderful it is to be alive.

It means saying "yes" to the things that bring you joy and satisfaction and "no" to those things that don't. In our culture, women have a hard time saying "no." At work it's called "not being a team player." At home or socially we worry that it's just not nice, and we try to come up with just about anything to say rather than a flat-out "no."

A socially prominent friend of Martha's recently was complaining about some of the civic duties that she's asked to perform in her small community. It's not that she doesn't want to serve and do her part; it's just that there are certain tasks she despises, public relations being one of them. So she rehearsed her avoidance tactic with Martha: "Here's what I'll say the next time I'm asked," her friend said. "'Oh, you don't want me to do public relations. I'm so awful at it, you'd just fire me right away.' What do you think?" Martha said, "You don't have to pay for your right to say 'no' with the currency of your self-esteem. Why put yourself down? If you want to say 'no' to public relations, say 'no' to public relations. Then offer your services in an area you want to participate in." The next challenge was helping her friend discover an activity she would enjoy. She had been so invested in disliking what she was being pressured to do that she hadn't given herself the time and chance to discover what she would like to do. Once she gives herself the time and chance to discover the activities that will be meaningful to the community *and* fun for her, her inner climate control will be reset to a more pleasant way of experiencing her life in this small town.

BODACIOUS WOMEN KNOW THEIR VALUE PREVAILS

The Now Economy is nothing if not an opportunity to get used to things changing minute by minute. During the New Economy we watched billions upon billions of dollars being made (often by the same people) using computer technology and the Internet. We heard so-called experts proclaim that the Old Economy ways of doing business were extinct. ("Business plan? Who needs a business plan? Got a good story? Great! Here's five million dollars for your idea.") And 19-year-olds smiled from the covers of Establishment business magazines such as *Fortune*. Why? Because they were the new moguls.

Then April 2000 happened. The first big NASDAQ meltdown. Then widespread shutdowns of dot.coms so certain they were onto a sure thing. And layoffs. And more layoffs. And then some more. If you key your self-worth—your own "brand"—according to the company you work for, a single downturn in the market could send your self-esteem spinning down the drain. You would be tempted to make the safe choice, the politically expedient action, rather than the authentic decision to protect your place in the company, even though your place in your own self-reckoning would be greatly diminished. And for what? A possible layoff? A possible downsizing? A possible closing of the doors forever?

The bodacious woman who knows her own value knows how that value fits into the marketplace regardless of how the market itself is doing. She knows that the quality of her work isn't lessened by the diminishing stock value of the company she works for. And she knows that the political or negotiating tactics of those she works with don't lessen the value of her contribution.

With a clear understanding of her intrinsic value, the bodacious woman is able to bring her contributions to a wide variety of markets. When hard times come, she simply repackages that value to appeal to the emerging new marketplace. As that one subsides she transforms yet again, all the while creating new iterations, new releases, of her original package, adding new features and technologies as they develop and as the market demands them. All the while, the original value remains intact, never lessened, always growing.

Bodacious women know both their value and their price. They seek out high-value customers, clients, and constituents and invest their energies in serving marketplaces that truly understand the worth of their contributions.

How to Make a Decision Like an Engineer

We make so many decisions, small and large, every day that making decisions is a strategic life skill. What you want for lunch, who's the best person to call when your computer is acting up again—these are no-brainer decisions. But it's easy to get overwhelmed with more complex decisions, to the extent that you want to cover your eyes and just pick a decision out of a hat. Which internal customer will you not satisfy because of budget cuts? What part of the company's new product will you eliminate to make the launch deadline? Using the engineering method of solving a problem makes thinking through a decision a little less daunting. You certainly don't have to be an engineer to understand this approach. And even though engineering seems like a science, at some point it becomes an art form just like everything else.

* **DEFINE THE QUESTION TO BE ANSWERED.** This can often be the toughest part because often you think you know, but perhaps it's not as clear as you thought. Do key others believe this is the question to be answered? Is there a truer question underneath the assumed one? Be specific and very clear on what you're really trying to figure out. It does you (and others) no good to solve the wrong problem.

* **DETERMINE YOUR GIVENS.** Write out the facts of the situation surrounding the decision—not opinions or feelings but objective data. For example, name the new company product, list all its existing features, note how this product fits into the company's strategy and what its expected contribution is, make a list of every internal and external person the product affects, and rate each feature in terms of importance by constituency.

✴ **LIST YOUR OPTIONS.** List all possible responses to your well-defined question. Sometimes it's helpful to think in terms of extremes and then move toward the middle. Also note your best educated guess on the impact of each option. If needed, do some research to fill in more understanding.

✴ **CHOOSE THE BEST OPTION FOR YOU.** Often the best choice becomes clear as you list all the options. If not, try ranking all your options based on what you'd like to happen. Either way, once you make your decision you can be more confident because now the trade-offs are clear to you. (Complex decisions always come with trade-offs.)

There are times in the Now Economy when you don't have the opportunity to be as methodical and thorough as an engineer. In these cases you could do an abbreviated form of the engineering method, or perhaps you feel confident enough to go with your gut. Going with your gut or intuition isn't necessarily bad or risky. Often it's just a more sophisticated way of arriving at a decision faster than the mind can consciously compute. If you later test your gut decision the engineering way, you may find out how your mind led you to your conclusion.

BODACIOUS WOMEN OBSERVE WHAT'S HAPPENING BUT DON'T JUMP TO CONCLUSIONS

I think all of us know someone who goes straight to the negative interpretation of any set of factual circumstances. She isn't certain how to interpret an ambiguous remark, so she finds the interpretation that will give her the most pain and make her feel the most insulted. It's a defense mechanism, I think. How much easier it is to duck the slings and arrows when you can predict the direction they're most likely to come from. This is also an easy habit to get into at work. And our interpretations as to what these circumstances "probably" mean affect our immediate security and future potential. Certainly, all these interpretations have merit. As they say in the CIA, just because you're paranoid, that doesn't mean no one's out to get you. But if we let negative interpretations drive all our experience on the job, they could lead us down the wrong path, causing us to jump to conclusions that are not only mistaken but also destructive to our careers.

Trusting our intuition that something is wrong is a good thing; trying to figure out why when you really don't know (and can't know) all the circumstances doesn't help. Recognize what's going on in your current environment, and try to see it for what it is on a strictly factual basis. Data are data. The bodacious woman resists the impulse to emotionalize data. She just observes, researches, and notes what happens and how, but not necessarily why. The *why*—or at least what you presume to be the *why*—could lead you into unnecessarily embattled territory.

Suppose you notice that there are no women above a certain rank in your company. It's easy to conclude that there's an unwritten but very effective barrier to women going beyond certain leadership roles. Or suppose that women aren't being asked to participate in hot projects in the company. It would be easy to imagine that somewhere there's a chummy little meeting where a whole bunch of guys are choosing from among their basketball pals or golfing buddies whom to include in each plum, career-making assignment.

Take a look around your work environment and really notice how things work. How open is this culture to women being able to work in the system just as well and effectively as men, if not more so? How do people get noticed? How do people get on special projects? How do people get to go to conferences and represent their company to the outside world? How is information shared? How do people get in front of their boss's boss or even higher up the organizational chart? What and who are the points of influence and power? A certain person? A certain title? A certain department that is currently getting all the research and development money? How do people get picked for the team?

Yes, business and careers often operate like a pick-up game. More often than not, the people who are included aren't necessarily the ones who can best shoot hoops or keep the golf game at an all-time low score. The ones who get included often are the ones who are simply *there*. And it takes a lot of bodaciousness to be there on a regular basis. You risk rejection, embarrassment, and frustration—all those hot red and orange words. But not being there puts you at risk for the worst words: failure, limitation, layoff.

And this, by the way, is the first and last sports analogy in the entire book. From now on, we're going to stick with business analogies. After all, we're all start-ups.

BODACIOUS WOMEN ARE CURIOUS

The bodacious woman seeks to expand her understanding of the world: people, places, cultures, philosophies, and occupations. She finds lifelong learning exciting. There is always something new to discover for the bodacious woman. She is rarely bored. She recognizes that learning opportunities are everywhere, not just in the classroom. They happen at dinner, online, on television, over drinks with friends.

She also knows that she doesn't have to believe everything she hears or adopt it into her value system. Seeking to understand other people's perspectives helps her be more effective, but it doesn't confuse her own sense of what's right and wrong for her personally. This is especially important in a diverse world.

The bodacious woman is not overly impressed by so-called experts. There's no such thing as a thorough expert anymore. The proverbial bar is always moving up on the latest information. According to a factoid I heard on CNN Headline News, in the next three years we will produce more original information than all the information produced in human history to date. New discoveries are being made every day, events are always unfolding.

Likewise, bodacious women don't wait until they're "experts," or at least feel as though they are, before having the courage to speak their minds. Your thoughtful, informed opinion is as good as the next person's.

BODACIOUS WOMEN TRUST THEIR INNER VOICE

A fun (well, actually pretty gross) commercial I once saw depicts two roommates, both female, one brushing her teeth. Roommate number one says, "Hey, isn't that *my* toothbrush?" Roommate two stops brushing for a moment, casually eyes the toothbrush, and says offhandedly, "Yes." As in, "What of it?" And then she shoves the toothbrush practically all the way back to her epiglottis and starts brushing her tongue with it. In a series of facial expressions that take roommate number one all the way from offense to revulsion and then Light Bulb! idea, we watch her brainstorm a business right then and there: one that helps match roommates up more effectively.

The advertiser was selling Web management services. But what we in TV Land saw was roommate number one listening to and trusting her inner voice, which was saying "There's got to be a better way to find a suitable roommate. Hey, I've got it!" No matter who we are, our inner voice will give us the inside edge to success because it will give us inside information that no one else has. The Bodacious Way is to see connections, opportunities, dead ends, and developments that other people don't. This is a creative mental and emotional habit that will give you an advantage in the marketplace as you anticipate commercial and personal opportunities before anyone else does. But it's also a trait that will have people wondering every now and then whether this time you've finally lost your mind. And there will be plenty of people—those who sincerely care about you and then the rest—who will express their doubts. And your best defense is knowing in your heart that despite all external and most obvious evidence to the contrary, you're right. The key is trusting that inner voice.

Maybe your inner voice is telling you what you *don't* want, without any real guidance as to what to reach for in its place. That one is guaranteed to worry the people who love you. That happened to me when I decided to throw away five years of engineering school (although you can never truly throw away any kind of education) without any firm idea what I wanted to do instead. I had chosen engineering school because it seemed like a good idea at the time. And my mother wisely pointed out that as one of the few women in engineering (this was in the early 1980s), I'd be practically guaranteed a high-paying job right out of college.

By my final year my inner voice just wouldn't hold its tongue any longer. Not that there's anything wrong with engineering as a career, mind you, but whenever I thought about the prospect of doing that work for the rest of *my* life, I got depressed. It wasn't right for me. It was always an uphill challenge, and whenever I got to the top of the hill, I didn't find the reward exhilarating. I was just grateful not to be sliding back down again. Not a good sign for a future career, was it?

There I was at the beginning of my adult life having just completed training that prepared me to do something I didn't enjoy. So without any idea what I would do in its place, I took a very bodacious step: I slammed a door behind me. I chose not to take one of the necessary qualifying exams that would position me as a legitimate job candidate. Not only did I slam that door, I locked it and threw away the key.

All my inner voice was telling me was what I *didn't* want to do, not what I wanted to do in its place. I had to let go of the thing I didn't want to do before I could grab hold of the next thing, a lesson I'd keep learning in my career and personal life. The trouble was I didn't know what that next thing was. (And try telling *that* to my mother.) But instead of feeling depressed about the uncertainty, I actually felt empowered by the fact that I had made a choice for myself. I wasn't looking forward to going home with the news, that's for sure. And it didn't help that I didn't have an alternative plan.

It probably didn't help my parents feel any better that my first job was an eight-dollar-an-hour entry-level support position with some no-name company. But it was definitely my first step to AOL and a career that far exceeded anyone's dreams and expectations, both in the experiences I ultimately had and in my financial future.

The more innovative we are, the more unique the paths we choose will be, and therefore the greater our reward will be. But, like it or not, the more likely it is that we will be surrounded by people who truly believe that we've just made the mistake of our lives. But we know different, don't we?

BODACIOUS WOMEN DON'T TAKE IT PERSONALLY

How much time do you and your coworkers waste trying to figure out "What did she mean by that?" or "What is it about me that tells people that they can treat me that way?" or "How could he give that piece of business to someone else? I thought we were friends!" or "How much should I charge her? I don't want to alienate her."

How to Journal for Discovery

We're not talking about your pink preteen diary with the lock holding all your secrets about your crush on Billy or how Sue hurt your feelings. And we're not talking about verbatim notes on all the details of what happened from the time your alarm clock sounded to when you found the covers again at night. We're talking real journaling for real women who are becoming really bodacious.

When I started grad school, we were required to keep a journal and provide a short summary every quarter. At first I found this odd for a business degree, but then I saw its wisdom. If we were going to be effective at helping organizations, we needed to deeply understand ourselves and the effect of our behavior. I began to discover how the simple act of capturing and processing an event helped me better understand my reaction and get past it to learn how to be more effective next time.

All you need is a notebook, a pen, about fifteen minutes, and an uncomplicated approach. I suggest you get a notebook that's just for journaling so you can watch your progress and so you can stash all your inner thoughts in one place for safekeeping. There are numerous ways to journal, but here's one straightforward technique I recommend.

* **DESCRIBE WHAT HAPPENED.** Choose an incident that has upset you. Even though you're probably full of thoughts and feelings about the event, first write out only what happened, not how you felt or what thoughts crossed your mind. Focus on the sequence of events and notable occurrences. For example, you were giving an important presentation to a group of marketing folks when John, who gladly gave you feedback on your analysis beforehand, is now publicly criticizing your analysis. You're fuming inside, but before you go off on John on paper, what else happened? How important was this presentation on a scale of one to ten and why? What key players were there? Did anything happen to you before the meeting occurred that affected your mental or emotional state? Write it down.

* **CAPTURE YOUR REACTION.** What did you think, feel, or do because of what happened? This part seems the easiest to conjure because most women are very aware of how they feel. But perhaps you've been such a good girl all these years you're not in touch with your raw emotions. If so, close your eyes, focus on what happened for a minute, and give yourself permission to feel or think anything that surfaces. Now is the time to go off on John. Did you feel betrayed? Angry? Scared? Wanted to cry? Did you think, "What the hell are you doing, John? Why are you trying to put cracks in my credibility?" Or did you think, "Oh no, maybe I didn't see an obvious flaw?" What did you do when he questioned you? Did you laugh a little, make a snappy joke out of it, and move on? Or did

you confidently explain the research source and cite similar references? Something happened inside and outside of you; what was it? Don't feel you have to capture everything; focus on the reactions that had the most punch.

✳ **CONSIDER WHAT YOU LEARNED.** Even if you don't get to this last step, the first two have provided a needed release on the event. Now you can focus on the rest of your day. But wait—there's more. In addition to being a safe place to vent, the journal helps you extract valuable insight for the next time around. You know there will be a next time, or something very similar. All you need to do is consider what your reaction is saying about you or others. Do you feel this way often? Is there a pattern you need to notice? Is it helping you or hindering you? Are you making progress on changing a mindset or behavior? What about others? Are you beginning to see sides of John that put him on your "beware" list? Or are you seeing a person of integrity with whom you want to align more closely? Who had the power in this situation and why? Who has knowledge you want to gain? At this point it's helpful to be kind. Your recollections often are a mixed bag of what you're proud of and how you wish you'd handled yourself. Other people are just as human as you and have their strengths and weaknesses. You shouldn't dismiss learning something negative about someone else, but you shouldn't have to dwell on it either.

Remember, becoming bodacious is a process, a journey. Journaling is a way to take what's already happening in your life and get more out of the situation by deliberately reflecting and learning. It's rewinding the tape and seeing what you didn't pick up on the first time. (Of course, after you review the tape, there's no need to dwell on it. Move on.) By making this a habit you'll become more aware of what's happening in you and with others in the moment. You'll start to take action in the moment that gives you power. You'll experience the wonderful process of becoming bodacious.

Bodacious women cultivate an attitude of healthy detachment, which enables them to separate intimate, cherished relationships (where things really do matter deeply and intensely) from more distant, practical-based relationships such as business dealings. There's absolutely no upside to bringing your personal feelings, sensitivities, and insecurities to the marketplace. For instance, Bill Gates once brought Steve Case to his Microsoft corporate headquarters (talk about a home court advantage—oops! sports analogy!) and gave him this carefully thought-out piece of insight, which to anyone's ears would naturally have been received as a threat: "I can buy 20 percent of you or I can buy all of you, or I can go into this business myself and bury you." Well, compared with the power of Bill Gates, Steve Case at the time was a pipsqueak with big ideas of turning a nothing company into something. If Steve had internalized that message of "You're nothing and I can squash you like a bug," there would be no AOL, maybe Time Warner would be owned by Microsoft instead, and the only book I would be writing would have been *How Fast Can You Type? My Life as an Uncredentialed Engineer.*

As we'll discuss later in the book, the Bodacious Way definitely depends on the power of relationships, but those are relationships that increase the power of *all* participants. To take things personally, in contrast, is to assume there's power in familiarity that will hurt us in some way. How much power do you give away because you think that someone has direct access to your stash of security, ability, sense of self-worth, and market position? Take something personally, and you're telling the world that this person has the key to your personal power supply.

As I moved through my career at AOL, I eventually moved out of the call center and took a promotion into the human resources department. About three months after making the move, I ran into one of the call center reps at a party. When I was call center manager, he was a couple of levels below me, but even so, he felt that he had the right to tell me he didn't approve of my career decision: "Gosh, Mary, I don't know why you left. You should have stayed in the call center; you would have done really well and risen up through the ranks. I don't know. It just doesn't seem like a very good decision to me."

What he was probably doing, in his own dopey way, was asking me for my thought process that he might be able to use for his own career advantage. But the message I heard was, "What could you have been thinking?" If I had taken the whole exchange personally, I would have felt that at the very least he was talking down to me (well, since I stand five feet, two inches tall, just about everybody talks down to me). Maybe I would have been offended. Maybe I would have reacted emotionally to a perceived insult. I mean, what, in fact, did give him the right to criticize my career moves? The fact that he was a guy? What exactly was it about me that indicated that I was receptive to such commentary?

Bottom line: It really didn't matter. I knew why I made the career move I did. And I also knew one more thing about him: He's an idiot. He was speaking in a patronizing way to someone farther up the ranks than he was, someone who might have been able to help him in his own career. Not very smart or politically savvy on his part. It didn't hurt my feelings, but I certainly filed away the fact that he wasn't very prudent in the way he spoke to people.

If you're going to get your hackles up by the way someone talks to you, the best way you can protect yourself is to at least consider the source. Taking things personally focuses your energy, emotions, and attention on all the wrong things. You spend your time worrying over perceived slights, checking yourself all over for digs, scars, and knives between your shoulder blades. Instead, you can calmly and rationally assess the situation, consider the source, and then move on.

By the way, operating in an atmosphere where you perceive things personally also costs you real money. When you perceive things personally, you probably also assume that other people do as well. Then your eagerness to please compromises your negotiating edge. One of Martha's friends once negotiated an hourly fee schedule from the offered eighteen dollars an hour to a whopping twenty dollars, when the market rate for her services is at least twenty-five, maybe thirty dollars.

"I would have asked for more, but I didn't want to alienate the guy," she said. This man was not a friend, he was a client. In fact, up until the moment of the surprise call for help, he was really a former boss, safely ensconced in her past. There was no personal relationship. There were no invitations to each other's house for dinner. And obviously he wasn't concerned about alienating her by low-balling his initial offer to her.

Nobody needs to get their feelings hurt in a business negotiation. If someone you're dealing with starts to get huffy and chilly, know that he or she is trying to use your emotional investment against you. See it for what it is: a head game that's worth a try. If they're stooping that low, it's probably because you have them at a disadvantage and this is their last-ditch effort to regain the upper hand.

BODACIOUS WOMEN GET OVER IT

Bad things happen, even to bodacious women! How we choose to interpret those bad things and integrate them into our life's story has a powerful influence on how quickly we're able to benefit from those bad things and move on in life. In her book *How to Succeed in Business Without a Penis*, author Karen Salmansohn says this:

> Women have to learn how to be better warriors. Basically, men are better at handling the remote control not only on their TV sets but also on their mindsets. Whereas women tend to rewind to mistakes and insecurities, and replay them over and over again, men switch channels until they find something enjoyable.

Mostly, men know not to waste valuable energy and time caught up in negative emotions. They know instinctively that this will only deplete and distract them from their goal. And men in business have one goal only: *win.*

Psychologists put it a little more elegantly, stating that the way we interpret the things that happen to us—our "explanatory style"—influences our ability to move on and even avoid depression. As women trying to make sense of a workplace environment according to the socializing rules we learned growing up (be nice, play fair, share, bring enough for the whole class, don't leave behind a mess for someone else to clean up, don't ask anyone do to what you wouldn't do yourself, treat people nicely and they'll treat you nicely), we constantly encounter people who very smartly discover that the more they appear displeased, the harder we'll work to try to please them. As a result of this never-ending cycle of frustration, many of us take on a feeling of learned helplessness: "It's all beyond my reach, there's no point, there's nothing I can do about it, the code is uncrackable, and the condition is permanent."

And that helplessness often leads to depression because not only can we not do anything about it (whatever "it" is at the moment), but we also won't stop obsessing about it. And in obsessing about it, we stop focusing on the aspects of life that give us the most meaning, joy, and feeling of power. Says Martin Seligman in his book *Learned Optimism: How to Change Your Mind and Your Life,* "Women are twice as likely to suffer depression as men are, because on the average they think about problems in ways that amplify depression. Men tend to act rather than reflect, but women tend to contemplate their depression, mulling it over and over, trying to analyze it and determine its source."

Well, here's news for you: In the workplace its source is the fact that everyone is out to (1) win, (2) keep their job, (3) make money, (4) get a promotion, and (5) *maybe* (I say "maybe" only because I've seen some people who couldn't care less about anyone but themselves) make a difference. If your feet get stepped on, it's not because you're morally flawed, unworthy, distracted, stupid, or somehow bad. It's just that you didn't get out of the way fast enough. Or better yet, it may be because *your* feet should have been one step ahead in the first place.

Get over it.

BODACIOUS WOMEN SEE BARRIERS AS AN OPPORTUNITY TO DO THINGS DIFFERENTLY

The bodacious woman knows that a barrier is really just an opportunity that someone will eventually profit from, and it might as well be her.

Remember that gross commercial about the toothbrush? If roommate number one was a nonbodacious woman, she would have immediately gone into barrier mode: "Look at that! She's violated my boundaries, and now her tongue germs are all over my toothbrush! How I'd love to get rid of this inconsiderate, revolting jerk. But I can't. I signed a lease, I need a roommate to help me afford this apartment [of course, we can safely assume she's making 78 percent of what her male counterpart is making], I wish I could get her to leave, I was really happier living by myself. But now's not the time to get her to leave. I don't want to hurt her feelings, besides she's just lost her boyfriend, they're laying people off at her job, she's under so much stress, it would be really selfish of me to ask her to move out right now. Maybe *I* could find a new place to live. Oh yeah, that's right, my name is on the lease."

And all her nonbodacious friends would have said, "Oh you poor thing!" Like a lot of help that is! Her problem hasn't been solved.

Instead, roommate one realized, "I can't be the only one with this problem. Hey! There's a business here!"

To perceive a situation from a barrier-oriented frame of mind is to take yourself down a very, very short dead-end road. To see things from an opportunity-oriented frame of mind is to take yourself up a highway with many exits and entrances, new options, new possibilities, new ways of considering the problem as a chance to improve life even more. It takes more creative brainpower, you have to keep your mind open just a little while longer, but the rewards are worth the extra effort.

BODACIOUS WOMEN FOCUS ON WHAT'S GOING RIGHT

No matter what our religion or philosophy, we eventually come across these principles: We create what we defend against. And we manifest what we focus on. So the logical conclusion is this: Don't focus so much on the things you don't want in your life.

In business management circles, there is an approach called appreciative inquiry, which invites participants to identify the things that are going right, learn from them, and then build up from that strong foundation. If you wait until everything is perfect before giving yourself the permission to move forward—before feeling as though you deserve good things—be prepared to wait forever.

Many women, especially those who were raised in harsh, judgmental families, live as though they are measured by some large, vertical, graduated scale, with the Zero Line situated in the middle. People who reside above the Zero Line don't even think much about this scale at all. But many women perceive their lives to be mostly below that line, a never-ending struggle just to achieve neutrality, with gravity, flaws, or even Original Sin always conspiring to pull them down if they're not vigilant. What an exhausting way to live! Always focusing on the negative, never giving themselves a moment's rest, stealing from themselves the little luxuries of relaxation and peace of mind that other people just accept as their birthright. Those who live that way are completely fluent in the wrongs they need to make right, without having the slightest idea of how fabulous and accomplished they really are.

Focusing on what's going right doesn't mean being in denial about all the elements in life that need fixing. But putting most of your attention and energy in the direction of the things that make you feel good about yourself will also give you the necessary self-esteem and staying power to address your negative burdens once and for all.

BODACIOUS WOMEN WELCOME RISK AND RELISH CHANGE

As I have already said in this book, the demands of the Now Economy are such that we must constantly deliver things, products, technology, ideas, and points of view that have never been seen before. This means that not only do we have to be equal to the never-ending demands on our creativity, but we also have to open ourselves to acceptance and, worse, rejection time and again. For every new thing and every new idea, we face the moment of truth: Will it be thumbs up or thumbs down?

Loss is not always loss. There is always something new to learn, someone new to meet. So what if you lose the beauty pageant? Maybe there was a talent agent in the audience who spotted your potential in a way no pageant judge could evaluate. So what if you failed to raise the necessary capital for your new business idea? Sure, it's disappointing to see your dream temporarily shelved, but if you paid attention you probably learned some very valuable pitching and negotiating skills that will serve you even better when the stakes are higher than you can imagine now. So what if you lost a promotion to someone else? Maybe it's time to go back to school or change employers. Or change departments. Whatever you do, use loss as a catapult for expanding your horizons, not for shrinking them.

But that means change, doesn't it? Suddenly you're challenged to be a bigger version of the person you thought you were. Suddenly you're not so easy to push around anymore. Suddenly you're having fun with more exciting friends and coworkers and working for a more dynamic company. Your projects are more interesting. You have increased visibility. Your increased visibility raises your personal stock even more, your projects become even more interesting, and you start having even more fun with even more new friends and coworkers who are exciting and dynamic.

Risk is good. Even loss is good if you know how to look at it. Change is great. Enjoy the ride. It can be scary, to be sure. But it's such a rush! And you'll get off at the end grinning.

BODACIOUS WOMEN KNOW THAT "GRATITUDE" ONLY RHYMES WITH "SERVITUDE"
Thanks to Oprah and Sarah Ban Breathnach, we've been hearing a lot about gratitude in the popular media these days. And it's good to be grateful. It makes us notice all the good things that have come into our lives. And when we do, it seems as though those good, positive things actually increase. Even the feeling of gratitude itself is something to be grateful for. Now that's bodacious!

However, taken to the extreme or used the wrong way, gratitude can actually become a burden dragging us down, especially with the feeling of indebtedness to the entire universe. For instance, although it seems supremely ungrateful to say "no" to a request for a special favor from a friend, it's best to make sure that when you do favors you do them willingly and authentically. When you say "no" to what you don't want to do, you're saving your time and energy for the things you do want to do and the people you want to serve. There is no cosmic scorekeeper keeping track of your balance sheet, but this is hard to remember when we're really, truly grateful for all the good things in our lives.

Soon after we were due to finish the manuscript for this book, Martha was scheduled to drive cross-country from Northern California to Cape Cod. As she was letting her friends know of her plans, an acquaintance from New Mexico showed up in her e-mail in-box, announcing how "synchronistic" it was that this plan developed at exactly the same time she needed to get her belongings out of someone's garage in a town three hours' drive north from Martha's California home. So would Martha please drive up to Santa Rosa, rent a U-Haul, load up the twenty or so boxes, plus desk, plus bookcases, and deliver them to her in Las Cruces on her way East? She'd pay her back, of course.

Martha's immediate reaction was, "This is a recipe for a big, fat hassle," but as she was writing the response e-mail to say "no," she found herself slipping into "yes" mode. After all, she reasoned, it was just an extra day's worth of details on her to-do list, and it would have been far more difficult for her acquaintance to make it all the way up from New Mexico. And Martha herself has benefited from the generosity of so many wonderful friends, it's the least she could do to help out this woman in her own time of need. It would be ungrateful not to, she reasoned.

Plus, she said in her most honest moments on the phone with a dear friend from their college years, "It just seems that if I don't do this, I'm setting myself up for a big thump on the head, a sort of cosmic comeuppance. Know what I mean?"

Her response: "The universe is not going to put a flat in your tire just because you tell someone to go to hell!"

Now she certainly wasn't suggesting that Martha use those exact words. But her point was made. The trip was postponed anyway, so Martha was never put to the test of using that new attitude. But I predict that a new opportunity will arise pretty soon. And she's keeping an eye on her tires just to be on the safe side.

Truly bodacious women have no shortage of generous energy. We give wholeheartedly, willingly, lovingly, and authentically. We don't need guilt or the possibility of a New Age noogie to open our hearts, hands, and wallets.

BODACIOUS WOMEN EMBRACE COMPETITION

Competition is a fact of life. Even though it's fashionable to go through life with the philosophy that there's enough opportunity for everyone (and in many ways that is still the truth, no matter what's going on with the economy), the truth is that at the end of the day there will be a victor on the field of conflict. And, unfortunately, there will also be bodies. Nonbodacious women who operate strictly from the standpoint of caretaking cannot celebrate their victory if that means there will be losers. It's not nice to be not nice. And if you win at the expense of someone else's loss, that's not nice. This goes counter to all our traditional roles: caretaking, being compassionate, nurturing, avoiding conflict, and seeking out win–win solutions in every circumstance.

But bodacious women embrace competition knowing full well that they're competing with bodacious others—men and women—

all intent on being the one left standing at the end of the day. In a truly competitive environment, winning is of no value or meaning if losing doesn't exist. The bodacious woman knows that beating someone doesn't mean beating them up. Does it mean the loser has to be killed, totally destroyed? Of course not. But it could mean losing a valuable contract that the company was depending on to keep it out of bankruptcy and keep its employees bringing home their paychecks. Or it could mean losing a promotion, or even a job. Bodacious women know it's not their responsibility to take care of the competition. Their first responsibility is to take care of themselves.

Both sides have the opportunity to win or lose. The opportunity to compete is the chance to give it your best shot, hone your skills, and learn new things, win or lose. Does this mean you should feel sorry for me if you win and I lose? No, it just means you came up with something better. As the loser, I need to understand why you won. And now it's up to me to ask the next bodacious questions: What does she have that I don't have? And how can I get that? What can I learn from her success? Do I need to adopt that? Do I want to adopt that?

The opportunity to compete is also the opportunity to review all the assets you do have, win or lose. In preparing for battle, you shift from a semiconscious awareness of your competence to being fully conscious of your competence. You are reminded of what you can do and that now you need to do it.

BODACIOUS WOMEN CULTIVATE RELATIONSHIPS FOR MANY REASONS

It really wasn't long ago that grown women were limited to establishing friendships with people they met at church, on the block, or in garden club meetings, wives of men who worked with their husbands, or the women who bent over the machine next to them on the factory floor. Now there's the freedom to create relationships with whomever we want, all over the world. Our new problem is that we struggle to find the time. In the Now Economy era we don't have time to linger over a coffeepot or casually call a friend just to catch up, whether we have a husband and kids or not. But we shouldn't stare at our computer monitors all day long, going from home computer to office computer without looking up. We need to seek out and cultivate the relationships that are effective and emotionally nourishing in all areas of our lives.

Our potential for relationships is no longer limited to who might be in our path. Thanks to technology, we're no longer limited to relationships with people we have met face to face. In fact, one of the aspects of the Now Economy that has been inherited from the New Economy is the emphasis on relationships, which I'll explore more fully in Chapter Three. Business is done on the strength of relationships now more than at any other time in history. In most Now Economy jobs you're being paid almost as much for who you know (and what they can do for the business you're in) as what you do. If your network of contacts doesn't resemble one of those airline route maps that appear in the back of in-flight magazines, you could be seriously limiting your future.

The sheer numbers of relationships that bodacious women cultivate over the country, or indeed the globe, don't detract from the genuine affection and warmth they share with their contacts. Fortunately, these truly authentic friends don't all expect to be invited to your wedding reception. You're not overly burdened by the bodacious Now Economy relationships you seek out, just as you don't expect a wedding invitation from the company vendor or new venture partner three thousand miles away.

Bodacious relationships support us because they know their place. Here are some reasons for the Now Economy relationships you probably have in your life:

PRACTICAL LIFE SUPPORT. In traditional, old-fashioned communities, if you want a barn built, you spread the word and suddenly a team of neighbors cum contractors show up and hoist the rafters in an afternoon. For the price of some cooling lemonade, fried chicken, and homemade pie, you got yourself a barn. Most of us don't need that kind of help anymore, but that doesn't mean we don't need help getting along in this world. The range of our needs extends from needing help with the simple day-to-day challenges all the way to the extraordinary moments when you're really on the ropes and without someone there to catch you, you'll fall farther than you might ever be able to recover from. On one end of the spectrum, whenever Martha moves to a new part of the country, one of the first things she does is ferret out new friends with pets. That way, she can always count on dedicated animal lovers to take care of her three cats while she travels for her frequent business trips and speeches. On the other end of the spectrum, when I left my husband and needed somewhere to stay, I turned to the support of friends who were willing to welcome me and my rattled life into their homes.

VIRGILS, GUIDES, MENTORS. In his literary masterpiece, *Dante's Inferno*, Dante is shown around the many layers of hell by his guide, Virgil. No matter where we are (heaven, hell, or anywhere in between) we need people to show us around and introduce us to the people we need to know to move forward in our lives (or in Dante's case, our afterlives). Tiane Mitchell-Gordon has been one of my guides. She introduced me to SARK's books as I was trying to rediscover my own bodacious self as my marriage was dissolving. And Tiane introduced me to Martha, who wrote *Find Your Calling, Love Your Life*, which I had also admired. And Martha, in turn, is introducing me to the world of publishing. And I am introducing Martha to the world of bodacious living.

OTHER AMBITIOUS WOMEN. This is the era of women's leadership groups. No matter where you live, you can find at least one or two local groups near you. These are gatherings of women who are ambitious, creative, energetic, and eager to make the most of the Now Economy, both in their personal lives and in their careers. There are many professional associations with women's chapters (no, they're not women's auxiliaries). And, as in Webgrrls (www.webgrrls.com), Women in Technology (www.witi.org), or Women in Film and Video (www.wifv.org), some professions have organizations strictly dedicated to advancing women in their field. For women in science and engineering, there's an online mentoring service to tap into at Mentornet (www.mentornet.net). These women, representing all levels of personal success, are a great source of inspiration, energy, creative solutions, and even partners and alliances for special projects and company start-ups.

Relationships happen for all different reasons and purposes. I'm sure you have some deep, nourishing, long-standing friendships that you pick up only now and then; you marvel, "Isn't it amazing how we just picked up where we left off years ago?" You don't need much from them on a daily basis, and they don't need much from you. Just a phone call now and then, or just an instant message on the computer once in a while, is enough to keep the bond firm and strong. Then there are other relationships that are a little more average but always dependable. You don't expect much from each other, but they're the ones who will feed your pets when you're gone or pick up your child from soccer practice.

BODACIOUS WOMEN NOTICE MOMENTS OF MAGIC AND SERENDIPITY

These days you hear people say more and more that nothing is coincidence. "Must have been meant to be" rolls off their lips, especially when something good happens. Bodacious women love this perspective because it draws attention to the small miracles in our lives. We say, "Wow, isn't it amazing this happened just as I was thinking about it?" or "I was just thinking about you, and now you're calling!" These are delightful little surprises in our life. Although there are many theories about what they mean, one thing is for sure: They make us stop and marvel.

But we also know that not everything in life feels so wonderful. A refrigerator magnet in Martha's kitchen reads, "When you want to make God laugh, just make plans." Bodacious women know that all the power in the world, all the technological wizardry that makes us think we're rulers of all that we survey, all the scheming in the world can turn as inconsequential as ash with one announcement from Above: "There has been a slight change of plans." What starts out as "slight" quickly turns into a life-changer. We're chugging along nicely, according to our own plan, meeting our year-end projections, our "where I'll be in five years" goals, and well on track for the twenty-year scenario. And then, suddenly, knock knock knock. The unforeseen shows up at the door. We're taken by the shoulders and spun around a few times. Then for good measure, we're knocked on our keisters so we can see life from a different angle.

Bodacious women know that not only do good things come in small packages, but they can also show up in exceedingly unpleasant packages. It isn't through the magic of science or the magic of television that wonderful gifts are created in unexpected moments; it's through the magic of "that's the way it goes sometimes." Through a traceable series of events, today's crushing disappointment turns into a delightful opportunity moments, days, years, even decades later. We won't really know for sure when the turnaround will happen, but the chances are good that something positive, some benefit, will arise from even most unsettling circumstances in our lives.

* * *

This is the Bodacious Way from the inside out. Perhaps there are a few you already relate to and are a part of your inner workings. If so, congratulations! Starting on the inside and making any internal shifts necessary to move us from a sense of helplessness to empowerment is the only way to act bodaciously out there, in the real world.

Next up: the bodacious strategies that will make you bigger, better, bolder in the Now Economy.

Staff Your Bodacious Start-Up Self

3

IT DIDN'T take me long after starting at AOL (back when it was still Quantum Computer Services) to realize that I was surrounded by a world that my Williamsburg childhood had not prepared me for. I wasn't exactly a country bumpkin when I reported for work the first day, but my matching blue pumps and "professional" vinyl folder would only take me as far as the interview. After that, it didn't matter whether I was dressed for success. The name of the game was to do the job.

This wasn't the corporate America I'd heard about. My expectation was of dark suits and white shirts with neck-choking ties for the men and foot-aching pumps for the women. It was the late 1980s, and this still was reality for many Dilbert-like companies but certainly not the one I'd joined. (In fact, when I did wear anything much dressier than jeans, and especially if I donned a suit, I was playfully harassed. "All dressed up today, Mary! When's the interview?") No, my coworkers taught me diversity, and we were a motley lot. There were tattoos and earrings in places I didn't even know could be pierced, there were computer geeks who couldn't coordinate colors, and there were folks who were trying the latest trends. (I remember one time when I felt particularly edgy wearing acid-washed red and black jeans after I'd gotten a daring new-wave haircut to match.) Judging from the looks of the employees of the conservative government contracting company sharing the same building, we must have been a sight. "Who *are* you people?" I imagined them thinking when we shared the elevator. "We may look like riffraff, but we're having the time of our lives creating an online experience you've never seen anywhere else" was my imagined answer.

All my AOL coworkers stood just as good a chance to do well as I did. They were hired for their passion for computers, for what they knew, for what they could learn, and more importantly what they could do for this bodacious little company with a vision that was already way too big for its britches. As ragtag as we were, each of us had been carefully interviewed, tested, and selected. Now it was up to us to make good. As the weeks passed, we were quickly ignited by that spark, that excitement, that passion to make this really cool dream come true.

At that time I didn't know, and was too unsophisticated to care, that AOL's senior leadership, also ragtag in its own way, felt the shared passion of building what would eventually be AOL. Good ideas are nothing if they aren't backed up by a mesh of relationships, starting with one irrepressible guy with a series of wild ideas (in this case, an almost unknown Bill Von Meister, without whom AOL would be nothing) and then moving on to the people he knows, and then the people they know. And suddenly you have a complex web of talents and connections. For instance, Steve Case was brought on board not because he was Steve Case but because he was a brother. In the early days of the company, Dan Case, an aggressive investment banker from San Francisco, was a hard-working favorite among powerful, older, more experienced bankers and investors. It was Dan who brought in younger brother Steve, an assistant brand manager for Procter & Gamble and based in Wichita. Sure, Steve had to have the goods, but a lot of people have the goods, *and* they don't get to be part of a bodacious start-up unless they have the goods and relationships. It was a relationship that put him on the track to hard work, fame and fortune, and then some more hard work. (And I don't see the fame and fortune coming to an end anytime soon.)

I knew none of this when I started, and I probably didn't care much. The boss is the boss, right? And at that age, who cares how he got there? By the time I started, all the big ideas hatched over dinner meetings, on barstools, and in front of the computer screen had morphed into Quantum Computer Services and would morph again into AOL not much later. Although we all took differing paths to get to this point, one thing kept us coming back (besides the paycheck, of course): relationships. Relationships to the dream and relationships to each other. And although we were still more than seven years away from the "official" start of the New Economy (1995, when Netscape went public), we were already building the wisdom of what it would take to thrive in all future economic eras: the technology of cultivating and sustaining relationships.

The Now Economy is a relationship economy. Everything is introduced, evaluated, negotiated, bought, sold, resolved, ended, and enjoyed based on relationships. The relationship is where the value lies. Relationships are what keeps people coming back and keeps them involved. Look at Amazon.com, for instance. The online store not only keeps its relationship with customers by providing almost instant gratification (the book, compact disc, or lawn chair you want delivered to your door the very next day), but it also gives its customers a rare opportunity to make a difference and get involved by posting book reviews and lists of their favorite books to recommend to other browsers.

Bodacious relationship builders know that the Now Economy is about using multiple pathways to connect with people. The technological advances of recent years are both metaphors and evidence of our demand for an infinite ability to make connections through computers, modems, phone lines, and organizations. But even in the high-tech environment, it's still about people. The hope for the Now Economy lies in the creative breakthroughs people make with technology, not the technology itself. Without that divine spark that only humans can provide, we'd just have a bunch of computers bleeping on tables in empty rooms. It's the divine spark that drives the technology to create the kinds of wonderful products, services, and relationships we have never seen before.

How to Be a Great Client

Have you ever paid attention to technology business terms and what they might be saying about relationships? For example, *client–server* describes how software (the client) on the user's end interacts with a more robust server computer on the other end to make an application run. When you click a button, the software tells the server, "Get me all the last names that start with *F* from the user database now!" It's not very pretty, unless you're really into command and control, which isn't the way effective Now Economy relationships work.

A more recent technology term provides a better relationship model. *Open,* as in *open architecture,* means that a shared language and technology allows systems to talk with one another and exchange information. Individual software applications and pieces of the system still keep their uniqueness while openly sharing valued information with others. Being open is so popular in the business world because it's more effective. All parties are directed at serving the client as effectively as possible.

When it comes to business relationships with consultants, we can apply these technology concepts. But, you may be thinking, "Why should I put any real effort into having a good relationship with the company I just hired to make my workload easier?" Because you'll get the most effective result possible.

The good news is that it's not hard to be a great client and get such results. All you need is to be deliberate about it, especially if you're in the "they should just do what I want" or the "I'm too busy to worry about this" mode. New ways of thinking and doing take some focus.

Here are some ways to maximize the potential.

* **THINK OF YOUR PROVIDER AS A PARTNER, NOT A VENDOR.** A vendor relationship makes it merely a transaction. It's like buying toothpaste: You need it and pay for it, but you're not very involved. Being a partner means treating the other party with respect, as you would treat any peer, thinking beyond the core exchange and considering what the other person needs from you to be successful.

* **EXPRESS YOUR EXPECTATIONS CLEARLY.** Be as specific as possible. What are the deliverables? What's the time line? What behaviors do you want? Let the other party know what success looks like to you. That way, they can target their efforts, and you have something to measure their performance.

* **SHARE AS MUCH INFORMATION AND ACCESS TO PEOPLE AS POSSIBLE.** Certainly it takes trust to believe that such information or access won't harm you. After that, give your partner as much as you can. Vendors aren't clairvoyant miracle workers. They need the same raw material you have to work with.

* **GIVE FEEDBACK OFTEN.** Be specific about what's going well and what concerns you. They'll keep doing what you like and correct what you don't.

> ✳ **IF A MAJOR CHANGE HAPPENS, TELL THEM AS SOON AS YOU CAN.** Changing circumstances are the norm in the Now Economy. When change happens, let your partners know so they can adjust. Sometimes it means their work is done. If so, treat them with respect. You never know when you'll need them again for your company or for a job.

Your Mother Always Said to Choose Your Friends Wisely

What I'm about to say here flies in the face of all good girl coding most of us have learned from the day we first heard "Now play nice. That's a good girl." And it might make you so mad that it will cause you to slam the book shut and put it down forever. I certainly hope not. But in the name of authenticity and full disclosure, I have to call it as I see it from inside the process: *Deliberately seek out new friends according to who they are, who they know, what they do, and what they can do for you.*

Sounds horrible, doesn't it? But you already do this. Now it's time to do it strategically. As you move toward a more authentic, bodacious sense of who you are and who you want to be, you're going to want to seek out other bodacious women whose skills, talents, and contacts complement your own. And they, in turn, are going to be wondering how to meet women like you. If it makes your inner good girl feel any better, you're actually doing *them* a favor.

Why does it sound wicked to be deliberate about selecting and nurturing some friends and ignoring opportunities for other acquaintances? Our good girl coding tells us that friendships are precious gifts that we should cherish, no matter where they come from. And that is absolutely true. But our coding goes on to say that any strategy on our part is scheming, cold-hearted, and socially materialistic. We're culturally instructed to welcome and nurture almost anyone who enters our sphere, and to do otherwise would be unkind and "unwomanly."

So what am I saying? That you should summarily ditch the dear friends whom you've decided aren't up to your new cool standards?

Of course not! That would be tragic and cruel. Genuine, sincere, dear friends come in all forms and speeds. And your childhood friend, with whom you have absolutely nothing in common at this stage of your lives, is still as much as sister to you as she was before you started this new journey to your bigger, bolder, more audacious self. But I would like to suggest two ideas to you:

* As you go about seeking new friendships that support your own personal growth, you can proactively plan to attract both men and women who can contribute meaningfully to your journey, and you can contribute meaningfully to theirs.

* As you manifest some of the changes you want to create in your life, you will discover that some of the relationships you once loyally called friendships were really just acquain-tanceships of convenience. And those are good, too. They have their purpose and place, and they're beneficial to both of you. But to expect more from them than what they are could be frustrating and even painful.

Bodacious friends are positive and optimistic; supportive and encouraging; adventurous in their own bodacious process; gener-ous in their positive wishes for you; curious, creative, and resourceful; and surrounded by other bodacious friends whom they can't wait to introduce you to. They treat themselves kindly and take petty emergencies and disappointments lightly. They can be needful at times, but they are never chronically needy. Bodacious friends give others the room and opportunity to be bodacious themselves.

People to discard or keep at arm's length are jealous and resent-ful of your good news. They make you feel uneasy, defensive, or tense. You find yourself focusing only on negative situations or com-plaints when you talk to these acquaintances. These acquaintances make you feel sheepish, selfish, or ashamed of your own growth pro-cess. They are more invested in sustaining their pain than learning about new worlds, new options, and new possibilities.

How do you get more of one kind of friendship and less of the other? Think like a bodacious start-up and do what Now Economy recruiters are doing to attract top-notch talent.

Strategies for Staffing Your Social Circles

What's your social circle like right now? Are you happy with the conversations that usually take shape in your group gabs? Are they about men all the time? Are they about victimization or complaining about work? When you get together, do you head straight for the mall? The movies? Are shopping, eating, complaining, or staying quiet in theaters ways to fill up time and space? When was the last time you created a great new idea with a friend and then took action on it to make it happen?

Heck, I like to shop, eat, watch movies, and even complain now and then, but a little of that goes a long way. And none of it helps you build a future that you can be proud of. It doesn't add excitement or hope to your life. And it doesn't expand your established ideas of what's possible and what's wonderful. Basically, this circle of friends helps you stay just as you are. And you're conspiring to help them do the same. That's stagnation. And in the Now Economy there's no future in stagnation.

Think of how you have found your friends in the past. My guess is that more often than not, you selected the best among whoever came along. Or you felt some kinship because you worked closely together or had something in common. And these are okay approaches, but they don't do much to increase the quality of the selection. This is very much the way Old Economy companies operated their general recruitment programs: They put an ad in the paper and selected from among the best that came along, hoping that the best people were reading the help-wanted ads. This Old Economy recruitment technique has huge limitations. Employers are tapping into the overall community of potential employees, most of whom probably wouldn't be a suitable match anyway, and they are trying to fill specific vacancies for the now rather than creating a bodacious future for the company.

In the February 1999 issue of *Fast Company* magazine, Barbara Beck, senior vice president of Cisco Systems, Inc. (one of the single most bodacious companies on the planet today and a leader in creative recruitment initiatives), said, "We don't fill jobs, we're constantly looking for people who can help drive the company forward."

A bodacious Now Economy career needs the support of a future-oriented and growth-oriented social life. Do your friends help you drive your own personal start-up forward into the future? Do they welcome your interest in helping them drive *their* start-ups forward? If not, you don't have to ditch the old friends, but you definitely need some new ones.

You have one huge advantage over Now Economy companies, however. As employers of full-time workers, they are limited to the availability of their candidates. This is a one-at-a-time deal. Once they've plucked a candidate off the market, that person is out of circulation, unavailable to other companies until he or she ready to leave the current employer. And if this person is a high-quality, bodacious performer, the current employer will do everything it can think of to hang on. This is why everyone's talking about the war for talent these days.

Your advantage is that you're not competing with anyone for the friendship of your candidates. When it comes to friends and social circles, we can have as many as we want. And we can share them with others. In fact, the more high-quality circles we belong to, the better off everyone is for the bodacious possibilities that arise out of the connections.

STRATEGY 1: PROFILE YOUR IDEAL CANDIDATE

High-quality companies have this one thing in common: They know that if you aspire to be the best, you seek out the best. You know what they say about birds of a feather. It's a widely understood and accepted principle that like attracts like. It's also understood that to find what you want, you have to know what you're looking for. That's why there's almost always a description of background requirements in each job description you see. If you're looking for the best, you must decide how you define *best*.

So what does a bodacious new friend look like to you? I can't dictate the specifics. Only you can decide these things for yourself, according to your values and objectives (which can be completely different, depending on which aspect of your life you're staffing up). Although there are no "right," one-size-fits-all answers, here are some ideas to get you started:

* People who are in key leadership positions

* Professional people who are in a certain age bracket

* People of a certain income bracket

* People who aren't impressed by money or material trappings

* Professional people who are active in sports

* People who are enrolled in graduate degrees in your field

* Professional people who are members of your religious organization

* Professional women who are mothers of preschool children

* Women who are successful in your profession

* Entrepreneurs who know how to attract angel investor funding

* Angel investors (birds aren't the only thing of a feather that flock together)

* Women who represent an achievement or personal growth spurt that you would like to experience yourself

What are the personality characteristics of your ideal candidate? At the very least, welcome into your life new friends who are upbeat, optimistic, creative, resourceful, light-hearted, and responsible. They will neither let you down nor bring you down.

STRATEGY 2: IDENTIFY YOUR FRINGE BENEFITS

The main difference between your own personal bodacious start-up and actual companies looking to hire is that with the companies there is usually a paycheck involved. And it's safe to assume that you don't want to pay people to be your friends. You have to offer something else of value. What's in it for them to invest their time with you?

This little exercise of self-discovery is important for two reasons:

1. Consciously or unconsciously, people (especially busy, in-demand people) have the tape of discernment running in their heads. With each choice to bring someone new in their lives, they ask themselves, "What's in it for me?" It could be something strictly emotional: "Being around Kate makes me feel inspired." Or it could be something practical and specific, such as your power within an organization or the power of the organization itself. If you're able to succinctly and gracefully capture what you have to offer, you'll get their attention sooner.

2. By fully appreciating the value of your fringe benefits, you neutralize your own "who am I to contact *her*?" feeling of unworthiness. Even making cold calls, which so many people dread, becomes easier when you know that you have something of value to offer and that you're actually doing her a favor by reaching out to her.

So what do they get from investing their time with you? At the very least, I would hope, they get a new friend who is upbeat, optimistic, creative, resourceful, light-hearted, and responsible.

(Here's a little reporter's technique from Martha, who as a writer spends her time calling strangers while researching books and articles. When you leave a voice mail message, state your name and then *slowly* state your phone number. Then you can launch into the body of your message. That way, the person you're calling can access your phone number later more easily and without having to listen to the whole spiel over again.)

STRATEGY 3: BE A TALENT SCOUT

Cisco Systems is famous for its unique ways of reaching out to high-potential candidates. One year it sent a group of Cisco employees to a football game between Stanford University and University of California at Berkeley, both high-quality schools with high-performing students and alumni in the high-tech fields. Cisco wasn't taking sides, though. It celebrated points scored by either team. At each end zone the Cisco contingent of employees waved placards that spelled out "www.cisco.com/jobs." On a separate occasion, the company set up a booth at the Santa Clara Home and Garden Show. It wasn't looking to expand its business into horticulture. Cisco reasoned logically that anyone successful enough to own a house and a garden in the infamously pricey Silicon Valley area must be doing something right with his or her career. And these were the people Cisco wanted to meet, so it had a booth among the trowels, tulips, and turf. (Not only does Cisco benefit from these unusual places for recruiting, but it also gets great media coverage.)

You can borrow inspiration from Cisco's example (although I wouldn't recommend waving a placard at football games: "Hi, please be my friend."). The idea is to put yourself where other bodacious people are likely to be. Like Cisco, use your imagination to beef up your bodacious staffing possibilities.

* Start a Bodacious Book Club at work, community center, or place of worship in which you read and discuss personal and professional development books. At the back of this book there's a list of my favorites that can get you started. (Visit www.gobodacious.com for more books I've included since this book was written.)

* Attend business meetings in your region. Most large newspapers feature a local business calendar on Mondays. You'll find announcements of local chapter meetings of your professional association, seminars, trade shows, and other events.

* Like Cisco, attend hobby centers of activity that are likely to be frequented by bodacious people: home and garden events, your local climbing wall, an upscale scuba diving club, museum lectures, and continuing education classes at your local college, especially business classes.

* Attend free lectures sponsored by your local bookstore, gourmet or natural food store, or other upscale shops.

* Patronize the best. You probably won't pay much more for the same service, and the connections you stand to make are invaluable. Word of mouth does wonders. So make sure the mouth can reach a wide variety of people. When Martha moved to California, for instance, she carefully scoped out the very best hair stylist in the Monterey Bay area. As a result of the rapport they built, the stylist recommended Martha to an attorney in Carmel who needed someone to house-sit his estate for six months while he was in Rome launching an Italian Internet start-up. And an excellent tailor whose shop is located in a high-end northern Virginia suburb introduced me to an investment opportunity offered by one of the most bodacious businesswomen I've met.

Remember, external signs of material success are only an indicator of possible bodaciousness; they could also be an indicator of a spending problem. Pursuing only relationships that show material success could net you a circle of friends who are merely materialistic or fashion followers or who are interested in *you* for the wrong reasons. And you could miss some valuable relationships among a more bohemian or more frugal crowd. You may get excellent stock advice from the driver of the Land Rover, but you may also get a wildly creative idea for marketing your business from the genius driving the ancient Subaru with dull paint. Or vice versa. Keep your mind open and your values intact.

* Seek out circles of impassioned, public service-minded volunteers determined to improve the world. Some of the most
bodacious people are in these kinds of mission-driven circles. Their self-esteem is fueled by the expectation that their
efforts will make a difference. It doesn't matter what you
volunteer for, as long as you believe in it. It could be Habitat
for Humanity (www.habitat.org). It could be Operation
Smile (www.opsmile.org). It could be your local humane
society. It could be local literacy programs. Or meals for the
housebound. Or battered women's shelters. There is a place
for your passion in public service. And that's where you will
develop relationships with equally passionate and energetic
people—the ultimate outlet for your bodaciousness.

STRATEGY 4: CREATE RECRUITMENT EVENTS

If you drive north on Highway 101 from Coyote Valley (just south
of San Jose) to San Francisco, you are not only commuting but also
taking part in the world's biggest recruitment event. The highway
is lined on both sides with come-ons from companies with jobs they
need to fill. Not only do you see more billboards stacked up along
fifty miles of highway (that's two hundred miles worth of billboards
if you factor in billboards that line both sides of the highway facing
south and then their back-to-back counterparts facing north), but
you'll also see banners hung from the windows of ultramodern high-
tech office buildings. There is even a company that regularly leases
the Santa Clara Convention Center and hosts hundreds of companies that are recruiting the highly desirable technically skilled talent
in Silicon Valley.

Employers and individuals used to do the same thing to attract
new talent: Sit back and see who comes along. And that used to be
both enough and appropriate, given the fact that both socially and
professionally our pools to select from were limited to our immediate communities. But no longer. As relationship recruiters we have
the world to choose from, thanks to technology and our growing
population centers. And so do our candidates.

But regardless of the infinite possibilities available to us to make valuable matches, we still struggle with the same old challenge: How do we make meaningful connections? Once again, follow the bodacious start-up business model. Do what the pros do: Hold recruitment events. But instead of seeking to hire these people, your objective is to expand your wealth of contacts. You don't even have to worry about placing them in any particular "jobs" or "assignments." This isn't about making practical use of people you meet. It's about strategically collecting equally bodacious people for future purposes.

Where two or more are gathered together, it's probably in the break room at work. Simply going in for your second cup of coffee can be a recruitment event. The coffee pot is one of the few places where you are likely to encounter on a casual basis a powerful, key player from another department, someone you wouldn't ordinarily encounter in meetings because the two of you work on entirely different aspects of the business. When you pour that cup, do you concentrate on the pot and, at the most, mumble an unspecified greeting that basically translates into, "Uh, you're in the way of the Sweet and Low"? A more outgoing, friendly, "Hi, how are ya? I'm [state your name]" could be the first step toward a fascinating new project, connection, idea, social circle, or insight into another department's set of priorities that will make you shine in your own work. Get a conversation rolling, even if it's a short one, just long enough to smile and stir your coffee; it could make a huge difference in the near future.

Create a women's leadership discussion group at work. Invite other women in your company to gather once or twice a month to discuss various aspects of your profession, industry, or company. Keep the conversation business- and career-oriented, especially if you hold the meetings on company property. Again, the emphasis is on positive, creative, resourceful discussions about the business that will move everyone forward in their careers. It shouldn't devolve into a complaintfest.

If you're not sure an ongoing discussion group will fly, try a one-time event to test interest and availability. That's what I did once at AOL when I worked in the human resources department. Over one summer it seemed to me that I was having similar conversations with my female human resources (HR) colleagues, who were spread out among half a dozen business units. My sense was that if we could all get together we'd begin to find the support and solutions to our challenges at work. So, I put together a chili and pool-hall "HR Female Thang" outing. (The last thing we needed was to sit around eating and complaining. A little out-of-the-ordinary recreation creates a common fun experience and gets the creative juices flowing.) I personally benefited by establishing a friendship with a Bodacious Woman that otherwise I probably wouldn't have developed.

Identify your counterparts outside your immediate company and meet regularly to address common areas of interest and concern. Freelance writer Vicki Meade discovered that she shared one problem with other full-time freelance writers in her hometown, Annapolis, Maryland: the feeling of isolation. Starting with just a few writers she knew, she began a twice-monthly writer's breakfast at a centrally located cafe. Attendance isn't mandatory, and the conversations range from one writer's new baby to another writer's new book to celebrating another writer's recent success to soothing yet another writer's weepy disappointment. Some of these writers compete directly with each other in certain markets, but more often than not they share job leads and business advice. Now in their fourth year, this is the one institution that these notoriously individualistic and independent individuals are committed to.

Throw a "bring one" party. Remember what we said about birds of a feather? If you are interested in expanding your network of powerful, positive, creative, upbeat, and resourceful men and women, I'm certain you know a few already. And I'm also certain that they know even more bodacious people from other business and social circles. Plan a party at your home or a local gathering place and invite all the bodacious people you know. Ask each to bring a bodacious friend they know. At this gathering, have each one introduce himself or herself, identifying what they're passionate about, what their special talent or calling is, what they're working on, and what kind of help or information source they're seeking.

STRATEGY 5: USE YOUR FRIENDS

Consider for a minute what the definition of *amateur* is. Most of us tend to think that an amateur isn't good enough at a particular thing to do it for a living. By definition, an amateur is someone who does something for the love of it, usually *only* for the love of it. The only money involved is going out, not coming in. But when we engage in that activity we love, no matter what it is, we feel plugged into something special: our best selves.

The main problem is that it feels so self-indulgent to do it (whatever "it" is), we often feel that we need a good excuse. But these are also gifts we can use to help others. And once we know what our friends do for the love of it, we can recruit them to put their passions into action. Often the activity that we consider ourselves amateur at reflects our creative energy to make the world a better place and rise above our immediate circumstances.

After Martha graduated from college, she moved to New York to do what thousands of postcollegiate young girl writers do: become a receptionist. Touch-typing and spelling were her strong points. Office procedure was not. And when her supervisor told her to "cc" a copy of a letter to Mr. Bigshot, she made the mistake of asking, "What's cc?" "You don't know what 'cc' stands for? You're freaking me out!" her supervisor said. But Martha had been getting used to that brand of unkindness from the woman, so it was just another bad moment among a string of them.

A few days later Martha mentioned to her boss that she was going to spend the next Saturday doing some work in a public darkroom, where she would print some pictures she had taken in Paris. And the supervisor invited herself along. Not being bodacious yet, Martha agreed to let her come. Once they were in the darkroom, her boss witnessed for the first time the magic of photographs emerging from blank white paper, and she was astounded. And said so, over and over again.

So Martha said quietly, "While you were busy learning what 'cc' stood for, I was busy learning how to use a darkroom." As she tells this story a few years later, she says it felt as though all the angels in heaven were high-fiving each other.

A lobbyist friend of Martha (and lobbyists are professionals at cultivating friendships) once told her that one of the best ways to make a friend is to ask that person for a favor. When you do someone a favor, the relationship goes that much deeper because you have made an investment in her or his well-being. By asking for a favor—the kind that only that person can do with that special flair because he or she loves to do it—you are retaining that person to engage in your life in a far more enchanting and bodacious way than before.

This is an especially powerful thing to do with coworkers. You're saying to them, "I see who you are beyond your job description. Let's take our relationship down a notch toward a more authentic level." Of course, you don't want to actually say those words. They'll think you're out of your mind. A simple, "Hey, that's really cool! Would you mind showing me how to do that?" should produce the same effect.

Everyone has a special talent or ability that makes life a little easier, healthier, or more enjoyable. That includes the people you know. Before Martha and I started working on this chapter, for instance, I didn't know that she can install dimmer switches and grounded electrical outlets. And she didn't know that I can create my own holiday cards using ink blocks, stamping, and original prose. Who do you know who can, or who can introduce you to someone who can do the following:

* Build a Web page

* Coach you for your next performance review

* Write an annual report

* Put together a public relations campaign

* Build a retirement investment portfolio

* Fix leaky plumbing

* Pill a cat

* Install a doorbell

* Frame a picture

* Throw a party

* Buy a car

* Negotiate bulk purchases

* Change a cranky child's mood

* Find the best travel deals

* Change spark plugs

* Make cold calls

* Work a room

* Hang drywall

* Hang wallpaper

* Do faux finishes

* Teach you the basics of golf

* Tune a piano

* Play hardball

* Conduct great job interviews

* Write a book proposal

* Give great haircuts

* Build a great basic jazz or classical collection and then tell you how to appreciate it

* Raise funds for charity

And let them use you. What is your special skill to add to the mix? Let it be known that you're also willing to share. In fact, as you start building your organization of bodacious relationships, take on the administrative role of capturing and managing all this great talent. Volunteer to keep up the directory of the members of your group. For those willing to be listed, include their special talent or skill. So when someone needs to have a dimmer switch installed or a salary increase negotiated, she'll check among her bodacious friends first.

Make this new gathering of bodacious relationships official. Just as college sororities are unified under some kind of identity, take the initiative and responsibility to gather up your chosen friends and coworkers, using bodaciousness as the common theme. If there can be book clubs and investment clubs, why not Bodacious Clubs? Meetings can be just simple get-togethers or can focus on a specific theme according to the members' expertise, say faux finishes one week and raising venture capital the next.

Be the first to open your home to a regular meeting. Or, better yet, follow Vicki Meade's example and find a cooperative cafe or other public space in which to gather. It won't take long before the group is established and can carry on without you having to be there every time.

How to Be an Empire Builder

By building a foundation of esteem and goodwill through-out your department, company, or industry, you're gathering a constituency of supporters with emotional ties to you or your perspective. Those relationships usually will respond positively to an attractive offer for getting involved and lock into place to support you when you have to face down a challenge to what you know to be right, fair, legal, or just plain good business sense.

Career bodaciousness is developing a reputation of being smart, focused on what's good for the business, optimistic, and well-respected throughout the many streams of influence that circulate throughout the company and your larger marketplace. To do that, you have to be an empire builder.

The little extra effort you take now to cultivate relationships based on goodwill, respect, and trust could mean the difference between winning and losing tomorrow or a year from now.

* **DEVELOP A REPUTATION FOR OPTIMISM.** You will achieve business and career objectives by focusing on what can be done, not on what can't. No one likes a phony Pollyanna, always chipper and looking on the bright side of things. But no one is comfortable around gloomy mood swings either. If you sincerely believe in the validity of the business plan or management principle, draw on that belief when times are less certain. Be the one people come to for positive, upbeat, resourceful conversations that emphasize what's possible.

* **KEEP DISPARAGING THOUGHTS TO YOURSELF.** Be known as someone who has nothing bad to say about anyone. This doesn't mean you aren't discerning in assessing people; it just means that you keep those thoughts to yourself.

* **KEEP OTHER PEOPLE'S SECRETS.** Be known as someone who is safe to confide in. You will then become the recipient of powerful information.

* **CONTRIBUTE TO INTERNAL COMMUNICATION PROJECTS.** If your company has an intranet or an employee newsletter or magazine, volunteer to supply it with

project, department, or staff news. Write a column exploring a specific aspect of the industry. Again, focus on the positive. Stay away from using this platform as a way to launch a negative campaign on controversial subjects such as politics or troublesome developments within the company.

✳ **INTRODUCE YOURSELF TO YOUR PEERS IN OTHER DEPARTMENTS.** A couple of times a month, have lunch with colleagues from areas you wouldn't ordinarily encounter in your routine work.

✳ **BE A CONNECTOR.** Who you know is very important. But who you can help other people know is also powerful. Be the one people go to for introductions to other make-it-happen players in your business. Recommend others for plum assignments you know would help them get noticed (and watch recommendations come back to you).

✳ **VOLUNTEER FOR CORPORATE COMMUNITY RELATIONS PROJECTS.** Your off-hours time and energy are powerful political tools. Picking up a paintbrush at a Habitat for Humanity project could position you next to a key executive who is stationed at the same wall you're assigned to. Volunteering to manage the holiday Angel Tree program will give you the opportunity to introduce yourself throughout the company as the person who is coordinating an important charity event to benefit children. Donating time and talent to a community-oriented project, such as First Night celebrations or a women's shelter—whatever is important to you personally (www.idealist.org is a good site to explore different options)—will help you meet other impassioned people from within your company and from the community. This is also an excellent way to represent the company in a positive way to the outside world.*

It's easy to find complainers in any organization. But optimistic, powerful, smart, ethical, standards-driven con-tributors are rare. Focus on being a member of this elite club and you will be marketing yourself as the person to trust and follow.

The Three A's: Now Economy Ways to Leverage Your Relationships

Grow fast. Grow now. Grow first. Toward the end of the 1990s it was increasingly obvious to Internet entrepreneurs that "speed to market" was critical. In fact, for a while it seemed that not only were all the words in the dictionary used up as domain names (some companies were spending hundreds of thousands of dollars to buy nonsensical words already snatched up by cybersquatters), but every brilliant new business idea dreamed up by a hot entrepreneur in his sleep under Silicon Valley stars was cruising the neighborhoods and visiting seven others. All those zzzzz's that floated up into the midnight sky from the terra-cotta rooftops of multi-million-dollar subdivisions were punctuated by idea light bulbs. Bing, bing, bing. All those sleeping subconsciouses were turning on to the same idea.

By sunrise, it didn't matter what the idea was or who had it; what mattered was who reached for the bedside phone and speed dialed the venture capitalist first.

---

* Habitat for Humanity International is a nonprofit, nondenominational Christian housing organization whose aim is to draw together the time, talent, and resources to build decent, affordable houses for those in need. Contact their headquarters at www.habitat.org or your local affiliate for more information. Angel Tree is a program sponsored each Christmas by Prison Fellowship to provide holiday gifts to children of inmates. To find out more, check out www.angeltree.org. First Night is the community-oriented nonalcoholic event celebrating New Years' Eve through the visual and performing arts. Find one going on in your town via www.firstnightintl.org.

The difference between the winner and the losers is that the winner reaches out to her other relationships and mobilizes her talent and power network. This is a bodacious alternative to thinking that your personal power is defined by the margins of your résumé, which tells your story linearly, from one job or project to the next. By following the examples of successful entrepreneurs and start-ups, you can blow out the boundaries of your résumé and create a multidimensional saga of what you're capable of creating with a little help from your friends.

As important as a great new idea is, its best chances come when you reach out to others, bring the powerful talents, passions, and finances of other people into the mix, and deliver the product to the marketplace as fast as you can. This is how AOL emerged from a distant third in the online services marketplace (behind Prodigy and CompuServe). At AOL, we didn't try to create everything ourselves internally. That would have slowed us down intolerably, and it would have limited our ability to provide the world with online content that is simultaneously comprehensive, useful, and extraordinary. And online services are nothing if not comprehensive, useful, and extraordinary.

We have to be comprehensive, useful, and extraordinary in our own careers to stay competitive in our professional marketplace. You can achieve this by developing relationships using the Three A's: alliance, aggregation, and acquisition.

ALLIANCES

You are probably the most familiar with alliance relationships. You create and operate within alliances every day. When you go to the dentist, the two of you are entering into an alliance to keep your teeth healthy. When people go out on a date, the parties enter into an alliance to create a pleasant evening with each other. When you retain a divorce lawyer, you enter into an alliance to make sure your interests are protected while you dissolve a bad match. When you ask your company's graphics department to design a brochure for you, you enter into an alliance to create an attractive, persua-sive piece of paper that will help you sell the company's product or service. So now that you're aware of this approach as a mechanism for strategically achieving more powerful objectives, you can riffle through your mental list of bodacious relationships and select the ones most likely to powerfully ratchet up your idea to the next level of possibility.

For example, shortly after AOL announced its acquisition of Netscape in the late 1990s, it launched iPlanet, a three-way alliance between AOL, Netscape, and Sun Microsystems. Each party was mature in the Internet space. The idea was to use the unique skills and abilities of each group to offer an Internet ser-vice deployment platform for companies that need e-commerce solutions. Netscape brought its pioneering browser, Sun brought its server technology (which powers 70 percent of the Internet), and AOL added to the mix its content and consumer knowledge. Today iPlanet is the choice of more than half the Fortune 100 companies, including seven of the top ten commercial banks, nine of the top ten telecoms, and a half-dozen leading wireless ventures. Now that's a bodacious relationship result!

How to Be a Great Consultant

In the Now Economy, whether you're a company employee or a free agent, you are *always* a consultant. You are always exchanging something you know or can do for something you want, be it money, power, prestige, impact, or recogni-tion. It's the way the world works, and lots of good can come of it, the best being that both parties' needs are met.

Keeping a consultant mindset keeps you customer-oriented, which is the best way to set yourself up for a successful relationship with your client. When it's all about the customer, you can be sure it's really all about results in the Now Economy. These are the techniques of effec-tive consultants:

✳ **ASK GOOD QUESTIONS.** Lots of them. Good questions are specific and pertinent to the situation. You'll need to ask some close-ended yes-or-no questions, but often your most valuable questions are open-ended and lead to a ongoing conversation with the client.

✳ **LISTEN, LISTEN, LISTEN.** It's more powerful for consultants to talk less and listen more. You may be perceived as the expert, but only the client can give you the raw situation-specific information to apply your experience. And listen to what's *not* being said. There may be an important reason certain details were left out. Ask more questions. Listen some more.

✳ **BE CLEAR ON WHAT THE CUSTOMER WANTS.** What are your clients' expectations? They may not know, so you may need to help them discover and articulate them. Be specific. The more specific you are, the more likely you are to satisfy their needs, and they will know it.

✳ **BE CLEAR AND HONEST ABOUT HOW YOU CAN OR CANNOT MEET THEIR NEEDS.** This is where integrity matters. Don't do it if what's involved doesn't sit well with your values. Don't do it if you don't have the necessary skills or knowledge. It's better to politely turn down a possible assignment, or even refer another possible source, than do a poor job. Find the work that was meant for you.

✳ **ASK FOR WHAT YOU'RE WORTH.** You might be so eager to get the work that you lowball your bid. Big mistake. Not only will you get less money, but you will also reduce your perceived value in your client's eyes. If you sell yourself short through your bid process, the client will continue to treat you that way well into the life of the assignment. It also makes it very difficult for you to increase your fees later.

* **CONTINUALLY MONITOR THE CUSTOMER'S SATISFACTION WITH YOUR WORK.** If your client is unhappy with your work in progress, he or she probably won't like the end result. Sometimes they won't tell you directly because of their emotional discomfort, sometimes because they aren't completely aware of it themselves. Watch for subtle changes in tone, less frequent communication, exclusion from meetings, or anything that's different from their usual behavior with you.

* **CONTINUALLY MONITOR THE LANDSCAPE FOR CHANGES THAT MAY AFFECT YOUR EFFORTS.** In addition to what your direct client thinks, keep tabs on what's going on with other people and the organization. Ideally, you can leverage changes to enhance the outcome of your project. At worst, if you're no longer needed, at least you saw it coming. If that's the situation, don't take it personally; simply move on.

* **BUILD ON YOUR PERFORMANCE.** As you build your relationship with the client and prove your value, build on that success by proposing more ways you can help. A chance event may play well to your expertise, or maybe you've noticed something all along that needs to be addressed. Proactively suggest how you can provide some relief.

AGGREGATIONS

The difference between an alliance and an aggregation is the power relationship. With an alliance two people combine their assets to create a third value element, and they share the power equally. In an aggregation, one person is the power linchpin, collecting and organizing all the other contributors. A temp agency, for example, is an aggregator. The owner of the agency collects the best available temporary employees and offers the combined result to the marketplace.

How can you be an aggregator? Suppose you collected your circle of bodacious contributors that we described earlier. And suddenly you discovered a huge demand in your community for concierge services. People are willing to pay to have their spark plugs changed, pictures framed, and so on. And you discover that your friends would welcome the chance to earn extra cash. As the key point of contact, you can market your friends to potential customers and make assignments according to the skill that's requested. You can earn extra money yourself by charging a commission on the value of the service, or you can do it for the pleasure of helping others.

Either way, you're functioning as an aggregator. Often your power in these situations is not about the money anyway. As people start thinking of you as a central conduit for important news and exciting projects, your power is in the positioning of yourself as the person who knows everything that's worth knowing—or at least knowing how to find that out. That kind of clout can take you far.

ACQUISITIONS

When companies engage in acquisitions, they actually buy each other or pieces of each other. AOL has participated in many acquisitions, but the two most famous are the purchase of Netscape in 1999 and the monster acquisition of Time Warner in 2001.

I assume you're not interested in buying slaves or body parts, so this model doesn't directly fit the relationship aspect of building your career. Or does it? You certainly can't buy someone else, but you can acquire the skills, knowledge, and insight they have in a particular area you want to master yourself. Perhaps you can even pay them to transfer that knowledge into your head. However, it's important to understand that you're not paying people for their time. That's an unbodacious relationship. Time is part of a life, and you can't buy a life. You are paying for the value of their willingness to perform a knowledge transfer, and you're paying for the knowledge transfer itself.

This is an important distinction, especially when it's you offering your knowledge to the marketplace. Emphasize that you are selling value, not hours.

The Ten Things You Want Your Reputation to Say About You

Unless you have a good reputation, you won't have the bodacious relationships you'll need to reach your fullest potential in the Now Economy environment. Because the Now Economy depends on creativity and imagination more than ever before, there has to be a more profound atmosphere of trust and mutual respect throughout any organization, whether it's the organization of your company or your life. This way you're kept in the loop of great ideas, sensitive information, and future developments that can affect your own interests. Back in my training days at AOL, for instance, I heard several times from a training consultant that our engineers told her they had some wonderful ideas for making the company better, more efficient, and more entertaining for our members. But they were hesitant to bring them forward to the managers, she said, because they weren't certain that the ideas would be treated with respect or that they would enjoy whatever benefits of ownership might come their way (recognition, the opportunity to personally implement their cool ideas, bonuses, and so on).

AOL's management philosophy has always been to give credit where credit's due and to reward initiative and creativity at every opportunity. Without that, the company wouldn't have had much to leverage. However, these new engineers came from different backgrounds at other companies and hadn't yet gotten the message that AOL rewards creativity. And I could see that we needed to market our reputation better by repeatedly sending out the message that it is AOL's philosophy to support and reward its employees honorably and consistently at every opportunity.

On a personal level, good reputations have been built in much the same way for centuries. No matter what culture or ethnic background we come from, the basic rules of honesty, dependability, and trustworthiness translate across relationships throughout the world and throughout time. Here are the ten things you want your reputation to say about you:

1. *You give credit where it's due.* In the Now Economy you're nothing without the support of other peoples' contributions, technical know-how, and creative ideas. Make sure you share the credit with your team members, and make sure your team members know that you did.

2. *You create a safe place for brainstorming.* People need to know that their ideas are safe with you, that even if the ideas are terrible, you'll receive them respectfully and kindly. People need to know that you believe there is no such thing as a bad idea, just a good jumping-off place toward better ones.

3. *You respect yourself but take yourself lightly.* Your self-respect will elicit respect from others. And your ability to laugh at your own moments of foolishness or mistakes will make everyone relax around you. (Just make sure that not all your comments are self-deprecating. That's a sign that you don't think much of yourself, which isn't true if you're bodacious.)

4. *You keep confidences.* As you move up in an organization, you will know employees' personal secrets and the company's trade secrets. The more you keep your ears open and your mouth closed, the more people will want to share valuable information with you.

5. *You seek out diversity.* High-potential employees and friends are found among every age, class, race, sex, level of education, and organizational position. You create a space in your life that will hold everyone.

6. *You're comfortable with conflict.* You see that conflict is a dynamic circumstance that can lead to even more powerful creativity. You don't lose your cool or get mean when the heat's on.

7. *You share information.* People can count on you to pass on interesting articles, books, and observations to help them grow in their own careers and lives.

8. *You try to assume the positive interpretation in a questionable circumstance.* When you're in doubt you can go one of two ways: pessimistic and suspicious or optimistic and positive. People feel safe with you because they know you're assuming the best of them. This doesn't mean you give up your discernment. If someone's dealings truly are shady, it's best to distance yourself from them, at least until you know more.

9. *You don't internalize, globalize, or catastrophize negative situations.* Sure, bad things happen, but you keep them in perspective.

10. *You're unambiguous about your principles.* When you put a stake in the ground, you mean it. You take a stand.

Bodacious Women Take a Stand

LIFE HAS a way of teaching us the really important lessons in stereo. When you don't pick up the message on one channel—say, in you career—you get an extra review chapter on a second channel, often some aspect of your personal life. The message to slow down, for instance, doesn't come only the morning you sleep through the alarm. It also comes in ever-escalating episodes: Your car breaks down, your workload is cut back, you stumble on loose pavement while running and are then laid up for a month with a broken ankle.

One lesson women typically have a terrible time with is establishing boundaries. As little girls, most of us were never taught how to say, "This is exactly how I want it." If we're at all particular about anything, from the shade of our lipstick to how we want our compact discs organized, we're criticized for being picky, selfish, or spoiled. Think, for example, how Meg Ryan's character in *When Harry Met Sally* was treated when she asked for her salad or her pie à la mode just so. If people love you, that sort of behavior is endearing or cute, as long as it doesn't embarrass anyone or cause them pain or inconvenience. Everyone else finds it really annoying.

The only time teenage American girls are overtly encouraged to lay down the law is on dates with teenage boys. Other than that, we're taught to please, to not take up too much room, to get out of the way, to serve everyone before serving ourselves, to not interrupt, and to be mindful of other people's feelings. The understood bargain was that if we treated other people the way we wanted to be treated ourselves, they'd notice and return the favor. No muss. No fuss. No risk.

In a perfect world, that may be true. But who lives in a perfect world? Setting boundaries was one of the lessons I learned in stereo. Because I grew up in a happy, healthy family where we treated each other respectfully and kindly, I entered my adult life unskilled at standing my ground in moments of conflict. I had never had my boundaries or principles violated until I was in my mid-20s. And it wasn't until I started to apply at work what I was learning in therapy in my attempt to save my marriage that I truly understood how establishing boundaries of expectation and respect is a problem for most American women, no matter how healthy their backgrounds were.

I was also learning that as a woman steps fully into her personal bodaciousness, she's going to start taking up more space. Those boundaries are going to start expanding. And she's going to have to protect those boundaries and establish new standards for how she's going to be treated from here on out. But we still have this issue, even in the Now Economy, when women have more opportunity than ever to be who we want to be. You'd think we'd have licked this one already. But it's still a core barrier for us in that we don't have the language or the skills to stick up for ourselves. As teenagers we may have been able to say "no" in the back of a car, but as adults it's hard to take a stand in our careers or in our personal relationships. It's just not a comfortable behavior for us.

If this chapter was written in the 1970s, I suppose it would have been considered the chapter on assertiveness. "Assertiveness," what a strange word that is. If you look it up in the dictionary, its definition includes *aggressiveness*. But most American women know there's a big difference. To be assertive is somehow okay, but heaven forbid we should cross the line into aggressiveness. That would be terrible because it would make other people feel bad. Because of the women's movement we gained responsibility for getting what we wanted, but we also had to get our wishes met in such a way that no one would object to our behavior. Not only were we responsible for achieving what we desired for ourselves and protecting ourselves from what we didn't want, but we had to do it according to a very precisely encoded dance and language, a code that no one really knew the key to.

If we acted in a manner that was less than ladylike, we risked being marked as a shrew or man-hater. If our well-intentioned attempts at being assertive were transparent, we risked being labeled manipulative. Not many women have actually been called those things out loud, but we all worry about it. We've been so afraid to risk a negative reaction that we choose not to take any action at all. And that's where we lose our bodacious power!

Even in the Now Economy, the warning messages of what a terrible reputation we'd develop are far more vivid than any actual instruction on how to move confidently and effectively in a coed work environment. What a hassle! For three decades, working women have said, "I'll just go the good girl route until someone figures this one out." Result? We still make less than men make, we're still underrepresented at the executive and board levels of corporations, and we're still hearing the absurd expression, "It's a man's world."

No, it's not. Work isn't even a man's game anymore. The Now Economy needs everyone to perform to his or her full potential. But to be able to do this, everyone must feel bodacious enough to say, "This is exactly how I want it. And this is what I don't want."

This is a lesson we can all learn. If you learn it quickly and learn it well (say, from this book), maybe you will be able to avoid getting it in stereo, like I did.

Get Control Over What You Can Control

It was my marriage that sent me into therapy. But it was my career that ultimately benefited from what I learned there (not to mention my ultimate personal well-being and peace of mind). I entered into both my career and, a few years later, my marriage completely risk averse. Feeling good about myself and my performance were the prevailing themes from my family life, and achievement was the main thing on my mind in my early adult life. I wanted a happy, healthy marriage, and I wanted excellence on the job. These sound like hopeful expectations that parents would love their kids to have. There was just one problem: I had an undeveloped ability to deal with conflict. But as it turned out, so much of my marriage was about conflict and violated boundaries that I sought professional help to learn how to protect my own well-being while working to keep the marriage alive.

I knew that I had to learn to establish expectations in all areas of my life, and that included work. No one at AOL knew what I was coping with at home, and I continued to achieve my goals on the job, which resulted in some very nice promotions. One of the most important steps up was taking over as call center manager in 1994, when AOL was poised for hypergrowth. In only fourteen months the call center went from 70 customer service representatives and 3 supervisors to 235 reps and 15 supervisors. They were a motley crowd, and paid the least of AOL employees; they were also the main contact with our members. We needed to keep them passionate about AOL. I also knew that our departmental hypergrowth was the first puff of a huge explosion within AOL. As we grew, the rest of the company mushroomed up behind us. Between 1995 and 1999 the company expanded from 1,000 to 12,000 employees. I knew that how we handled the call center hypergrowth was a test of how the company would handle the hypergrowth needed to capture the lead in the online services market. The heat was on.

Remember what I said about learning in stereo? One month after taking the call center manager job, I left my husband for the first time (the boundary lesson took a second time to really take hold). I had begun collecting the courage to say, "No more." No more harsh criticism, no more unrealistic expectations, no more unfair demands, no more fear. After one particular counseling session, I went home and watched as my husband wound himself up for a fight. Time seemed to go in slow motion as I saw what was about to happen. So I got up and ran, accidentally leaving my keys on the kitchen counter. I knew retrieving them would be a mistake. So feeling like a fugitive, I called a friend from a neighbor's and set about starting my own personal hypergrowth.

I was learning to be a leader of my own life. And that fed into learning how to be a leader at work. And work continued to be frantic; nothing stopped just because I was going through a personal crisis. When I had taken over the call center, everything was in chaos. We were constantly adding new customers, growing more quickly than we could handle the added business. As a result, we had more calls and more customer requests than we could easily manage. With the added demand, there was added stress. Our reps faced an ongoing stream of calls waiting to be answered. And most of those calls were from tense customers with a question or a problem, impatient after waiting on hold for so long. There was a pervasive feeling throughout the department that we couldn't do anything about it. All we could do, according to the culture, was hire as many people as fast as we could to replace those who burned out. Throwing bodies on the problem just wasn't an acceptable solution.

So I put my first stake in the ground and did something that would seem obvious to anyone from the outside but was a huge culture shift within: I established standards and insisted that we keep them.

I knew we couldn't control everything, but I also knew that there were certain aspects of the work that were within our control, even if it meant making our customers stay on hold a little while longer. We needed to give our people breaks to recharge, we needed to create schedules that worked better, we needed to establish quality and attendance standards, and we needed to invest in the employees by giving them training, one-on-one feedback, and team meetings so we could keep them informed about company developments.

And we needed to fire employees who couldn't or wouldn't perform according to standards, the least of which was showing up to work on time.

Well, at first people were shocked. We had had attendance policies before, but they were never enforced. And we were suffering the consequences—or lack thereof. For example, if a call center rep was a mere 15 minutes late to his or her shift, that meant three customers' calls went unanswered. If ten people were late, that meant thirty customers were backed up, a jam quickly compounded, and we'd never get caught up. We reinstituted our attendance policies, announcing that we would be tracking attendance and that we were serious this time. When people didn't measure up, we would let them know and give them a warning. But those who couldn't cope were gone before long.

Over a short period of time, that expectation became part of the department's culture. We couldn't afford to lose valuable employees, and we did everything we could to keep them. So it was quickly understood that if you were fired, you'd really earned it. Almost right away, the mood of the place changed. There was a higher consistency in work quality. People actually liked coming to work. There was more mutual respect and far more camaraderie, and reps recommended friends for openings.

And in the evenings I spent the next year going to counseling and sleeping in the spare bedroom in a friend's townhouse.

Why Bother?

Sometimes it feels like more trouble than it's worth, doesn't it? A little boundary here, snip snip. A little principle there, snip snip. What's the big deal? After a while, those boundaries add up. You've heard the expression "Nature abhors a vacuum," right? People also rush in to fill up a soft space you might have created by allowing a boundary to get mushy. Try this experiment the next time you're at the supermarket. Before paying for your groceries, move all the way down to the end of the cashier station, to the work surface where baggers load your purchases. Then try to return to your spot at the cash register. You'll find that the person behind you is already standing there. Or his or her cart is now taking up that space.

Next time you're first in line at a red light, let your car inch forward just a little bit (not so much that you're in the intersection) and keep an eye on the car behind you. It will move forward too.

It's nothing to take personally. These folks aren't even thinking. They're just moving along, filling in the space that's left in front of them. And space in the supermarket line or at the red light is hardly anything to obsess about. But it's a perfect illustration of the principle that if you're not mindful of your physical or emotional boundaries, you'll sacrifice your bodacious margins to others, whether they willfully invade your space or not.

Taking a stand at work is not just protective. It's bodacious.

Taking a stand establishes trustworthiness: By delineating your boundaries, you tell people what to expect of you. Not too long after I took over the call center manager position, I asked one of the reps how I was regarded on the floor. "Some of them don't like you, Mary," she said. "But they respect you because you're fair." What the staff had perceived as fair was really the consistency I had installed in the department. And that consistency was possible because I had decided what the rules were going to be, announced them to everyone, and then stuck by them. In return, I received respect and then I received trust.

Taking a stand puts other people on notice not to play games with your career: Your career is your territory, and only you can be fully

responsible for its progress. Only you can be responsible, ultimately, for your effectiveness. The Bodacious Woman seeks a
career path that gives her the power, clout, and autonomy to perform to her fullest potential. By taking a stand and not letting anyone inappropriately try to manage your performance, you are
telling your coworkers that you expect to be treated respectfully
and professionally, allowed to do what you do best.

*Taking a stand positions you as someone who will take effective action
for the sake of the company:* When you are known for being serious
about your principles, you develop a network of eyes, around the
organization that will slip you valuable pieces of information that
you can use to make a positive difference. That happened to me
once when I was alerted of an obscene voice mail by a direct
report. Not only was this inappropriate, it was also a form of
harassment, which added to the employee's already questionable
performance. And this resulted in my having to fire a person who
had started at AOL the exact same time I had.

There are various degrees of termination at AOL, starting with
a friendly agreement to part ways and ending with "Leave immediately and never come back." This guy was never to be allowed
on the property ever again. Ever. Period.

But his association with AOL was important to his self-esteem,
and he couldn't bear to be separated from us. So instead of trying to
reapply (which would have been futile, and he knew it), he got a job
with an independent AOL content partner, which had established
offices in the headquarters building. His new employer had no idea
that he had this restriction, and AOL management had no idea that
he was back until someone who knew him saw him. Although by this
time I had left the call center to work in human resources, the person who saw the offender felt that he could confide in me and that
I would take action, which I did. We couldn't fire the offender
because he wasn't working for us. But with a couple of well-placed
phone calls, we let our content partner know that this guy was pro-
hibited from being on AOL property. The issue was addressed, and
the problem was solved. But it wouldn't have happened that way if

my informant didn't trust me to take action on behalf of the principles of AOL and keep his own name off the record.

Taking a stand saves time: When you're clear and consistent about your principles, the people you work with are better able to anticipate what holds value for you. This is especially important when you're in a leadership position working to establish a self-managing team. When your team members are certain of your priorities and boundaries, you can dedicate more of your time and effort to making progress instead of rehashing old principles and guidelines.

Taking a stand reminds you what's important: By consistently reviewing and enforcing your boundaries, you are also reinforcing your own sense of self-worth. By allowing even the smallest violations pass without comment, you're telling your subconscious that your feelings aren't as important as the feelings of others. Once that process is set into motion, it's all the more difficult to reclaim your principles and reverse the trend.

Taking a stand adds to your stature as a senior player: When you think about it, only support staff are officially paid not to take a stand. They're paid to say "yes" and then go and do. (However, I have known exceptional support staff who are bodacious in taking a stand and therefore take a far more potent leadership role than they are usually paid for. I have also known "yes men" in the executive offices, and I suppose they're being paid for that, too.) Because so few women still have the nerve to speak up for themselves and their perspectives, taking a stand is still considered a masculine tactic. As a result, men admire and respect it, and once you're regarded as someone who consistently gets results, you will be included in a more elite group.

Don't Let This One Slide

It's up to you to decide at what point you're going to put your foot down. No one can tell you exactly how or when. But you'll know where that point is, even if it means facing the possible consequence of putting your relationship with your employer at risk. You'll know when you're feeling violated. You'll know when you're feeling used. You'll know when it's time to push back. And it might be just a small moment, but it's the moment when you change forever.

Workwise, for me that time came about six months after I was passed over for a promotion and my new boss had been hired from the outside. Distracted by other projects (the acquisition of CompuServe, for example), he left me alone during that period, allowing me to do unsupervised what I had already been doing unsupervised for several years before he came onboard. One day I sent out an e-mail to a round of colleagues asking for their input on a project. Of course, my boss was on the list. I got the suggestions I expected from others, but from my boss I got an e-mail that was full of command and control. After six months of leaving me alone, suddenly he was in my e-mail in-box telling me what to do. I was just asking for input, but he was suddenly giving me orders. I knew a violation had happened, and I knew exactly what it was about: He suddenly had time on his hands and decided to start sniffing around in my business.

The next morning we met in my office and I said, "You remember that e-mail you sent me last night? I've got to be honest, it sounded like you were telling me what to do. There's one thing I can't stand, and that's being told what to do."

If there was anyone in the world at that moment who had the right and mandate to tell me what to do, it was him. And I respected his positional power to do just that. But I had also had years of autonomy, working with and for managers who recognized my ability to figure things out and take the initiative to get it done without micro-management. So I added, "I've been in this role for several years now. And although you can tell me what to do and I will respect that, you should know that I will look for another situation to be in."

His response: "But I have my strong opinions." To which I responded, "That's fine, I welcome strong opinions. I want to hear your point of view. I definitely believe that with lots of input I can create a more effective result. But in the end, *I'm* responsible for what happens."

From that moment, he respected my ability and need to work without a heavy hand. I felt proud that I put a line in the sand. One benefit was that I got the behavior I wanted from him. But the longer-lasting benefit was that I learned yet again that although risk comes with dangers of losing a job, it also comes with rewards. And the risk of taking a stand often is rewarded with actually being able to keep the job you love.

Trust Your Instincts, Be Yourself, and Check With a Friend

Taking a stand isn't an exact science. The outcome of that moment of truth often depends on timing and the righteousness of your cause. Sometimes the best advocate for taking a stand is your gut feeling. It may seem illogical, but it's not; you just don't see the logical explanation at that moment. If something feels wrong, something is wrong. You may not know exactly *what* is wrong, but you know that it is wrong. Don't doubt your instincts just because the evidence isn't immediately obvious.

Even using the word *instincts* was a stretch for me in the early days. I used to be very deliberate about what I called my female vocabulary. My education in engineering, a male-dominated field of study, combined with my "don't show any emotion if you want to get respect as a woman" belief, taught me to put such expressions as "I feel" on ice. I used language such as "I think" (and, if I was daring, "I believe") that reflected more rational and logical realms—areas of thinking commonly associated with male thinking, although most of us know neither gender has a lock on rational thinking. But I was still hyperaware of my femininity in a male-dominated environment.

In the early years I actually felt embarrassment in bringing my femaleness into the workplace. The behavior code was "play like a boy, act like a boy." (This attitude prevails in many high-tech companies. When you think of the toys and blow-off-steam activities in Now Economy companies, you think of male-oriented games: foosball tables, video games, and skateboard ramps. The fact that a company has those games sometimes is mentioned in employment ads as an additional attraction.) I didn't want to broadcast my femaleness at all. I wore jeans, chinos, and other loose-fitting clothing to hide my female curves. I certainly didn't act in what I would have called a female way: giggly or silly. I didn't even like going to the bathroom with my purse. I thought it was some big signal, like a neon light over my head, "Period! Period! Period!"

I didn't care what the women thought; I was worried about what the men thought. And the joke was, of course, on me. They weren't thinking about it! But I was so caught up in neutralizing who I was that I was also out of touch with a basic principle of being true to myself. As time went on, I discovered that my femaleness was my asset, a strength, not a cause for embarrassment. That's when I learned to trust my instincts, to claim the mysterious, immeasurable vocabulary of feelings. And I started using those feelings in my environment at work. They are my friend. Of course, I may not react to them immediately, and I may not necessarily know what they mean right away, either. But I discovered that whether I was mad or sad, ready to cry or red with anger, was important information that warranted my attention.

This is when trusted friends are an important resource: when your emotions are so strong that you can't see the facts clearly. Often friends can see things from an objective distance. They can hear you out, consider the details, and tell you why you're feeling the way you're feeling, without necessarily telling you what you should do about those feelings. Ultimately, that's still up to you.

A Little Testosterone Goes a Long Way

After being surrounded by mainly guys in engineering school and the first seven years at AOL, I've come to appreciate some of the ways men operate that serve them well in business. I'm not about to adopt all of their behaviors because I can't do it as well as they can (they have the born-with-it advantage) and I like many of my female attributes. Still, a little testosterone goes a long way. Just a bit of their approach can help free us to be the bodacious women we want to be.

Here are some of men's "testy" behaviors that women could benefit from stealing:

> ✳ **LET NEGATIVE WORDS BOUNCE OFF.** Men have a wonderful ability to not allow negative "sticky notes" to, well, stick to them. "John, that report is missing a key conclusion." "What do you mean you can't get it done by Friday, Frank? Don't you know how important this account is?" These kinds of words seem to roll off their backs. I say "seem" because I'm sure they have some impact, but men don't show it. They don't absorb these words into their very being, as many women do. Instead, they decide whether the words have merit. If they do, it's a problem to solve but not a huge character flaw that requires counseling.

> ✳ **SAY NO WITHOUT GUILT.** This is one of my favorites. Men aren't nearly as concerned about making others happy as they are about taking care of their needs. Sound selfish? It doesn't have to be. If they were so concerned about everyone else's needs, they couldn't provide—financially, emotionally, or otherwise—for those they care most about. They'd disperse their efforts to the point that they'd be ineffective. The only way to keep focused is to freely say "no" to anyone or anything that doesn't enable you to achieve what's most important to you.

> ✳ **ACT AS IF YOU KNOW WHAT YOU'RE DOING EVEN IF YOU'RE NOT QUITE SURE.** I have to admit, I was alarmed and disturbed when I first saw this behavior. "They are lying through their teeth!" I thought. Then I took a

second look. These men were delivering on their promises. And they acted so confident that I assumed they knew this stuff like the back of their hands. But a male friend revealed to me that he didn't always know for sure how he was going to accomplish a project; he just believed he'd figure it out. Whatever knowledge he didn't have he got, and he used his smarts to apply it as needed. I finally realized it was a matter of believing in yourself and being resourceful. Lying had nothing to do with it.

✳ **FEEL FREE TO TALK ABOUT YOURSELF AND BELIEVE HOW WONDERFUL YOU ARE.** I immediately think of a couple on their first date. He wants to impress, so he tells her all the wonderful things about himself so she'll admire him. Sometimes he's successful, sometimes not, but one thing I do admire is that he's willing to proudly show his colorful feathers. That's risky; he might be rejected. But he knows he'll never be recognized if he doesn't try.

✳ **DON'T READ MUCH PAST WHAT'S THERE.** Most women think men are a bit dull and simplistic not to notice all the hidden messages in Sue's tone or David's words. And compared with the typical female radar, they are. But this so-called ignorance also allows men to not get caught up in all the energy-draining sludge of what-ifs and hurt feelings. As women we can't completely go against our natural wiring, but we can stop it from working against us. Differentiate between the facts of a situation and what else you intuitively pick up on that may also be true. Don't jump to conclusions about these ambiguous items, just keep them on the list of possibilities. Above all else, mentally move on to the next thing.

Stand by Your Stand

It's one thing to start a new job fresh, with new relationships to create, with your new resolutions to stand up for what you believe in. It's another thing to take what you're learning into the system you're already in and try to make a major change in the culture of your current relationships. You are suddenly breaking the unspoken agreement that you will behave according to a code even when your principles are being compromised. Suddenly, you're behaving more forcefully, more assertively. You're speaking up more and drawing the line more. When you suddenly start drawing the line, other people will feel as though you're drawing the line in *their* territory. Suddenly they can't move about so freely around you anymore. That's going to be uncomfortable for them, and that's when you can expect to get some push-back. You may encounter resistance and resentment. But you will certainly meet up with people who don't believe you are committed to this new way of taking a stand for your principles. And you will experience some counteraction designed to test your resolve.

At least nine different personalities may emerge from your associates in reaction to your new spine:

1. *The caretaker:* This person will express such concerns as, "You haven't been yourself lately. Are you all right? You've been pretty edgy and people have been wondering if there is something wrong at home." Of course you're edgy. You're practicing a new skill, and you're concerned that you might be doing it too forcefully, offending people unnecessarily when all you want to do is establish clearer boundaries and standards for how you want to be treated. The caretaker may be a true friend who is sincerely concerned with your welfare and worried about your change in behavior. Or the caretaker might be a false friend who is just gathering data to somehow leverage against you. Share your process with true friends, but be cautious with sudden friends who ask prying questions.

2. *The gossip:* This person may come off as a friend, but offers "helpful insights" into how you're being perceived and received by others. Such messages as "Everybody says so" or "There's been talk" are never positive and encouraging. Beware. Don't share.

3. *The distracter:* This person tries to seize control over the conversation by saying things like, "What you should really care about is. . . ." You'll hear this when you're trying to express an objection to something that person did or said. He or she is trying to take you off point by making you feel that you are somehow wrong to express your feelings or opinion.

4. *The planter:* This person handles discomfort by planting seeds of doubt in your mind about your position. You will hear, "Are you sure?" "Did you do sufficient reading on the subject?" "According to my many more years of experience (conversations, insider information, etc.), the better way to interpret this situation is. . . ." Perhaps in Old Economy environments, length and depth of experience was the final authority on a subject, but there is so much that is new in the Now Economy. Your thoughtful perspective is as valid as anyone's, no matter how junior you are in the company.

5. *The fisher:* This person will put you on the defensive by aggressively demanding to know more information about your area of concern. You'll hear questions such as, "Who told you to say this to me?" "What else do you know?" "What are other people saying?" These kinds of questions and demands are designed to escalate your own tension and rattle you. Stay calm, stay focused on your message. Answer only the questions you want that are pertinent and unemotional. If you feel yourself getting rattled, postpone the rest of the conversation until you've calmed down. Or don't even pick it up again if you don't want to.

6. *The fidgeter:* This is another rattling maneuver. You're tense. You're uncertain. You're trying to express your concerns clearly and unemotionally. In the meantime, the person you're talking to keeps looking at her watch, shuffling and reorganizing papers, glancing out the door. All this activity is making you feel rushed and unheard. Stand your ground. Stay focused. And take your time. Their relief from being uncomfortable can wait.

7. *The cajoler:* The cajoler is one of the most diabolical personalities. This person is someone whom you've confided in before, someone whose opinion you trust, a boss or a mentor whose guidance you have sought in the past. This is usually a one-down relationship, with you in the down position. It's not uncommon to outgrow your mentors and advisors. In fact, you're expected to. But many superiors feel insecure when they see you establish your own rules and assert independence. Then you will hear expressions such as "Aw, come one, you don't really mean that" or "You sure aren't the sweet woman I thought I knew." Or they will refer back to a privileged piece of information that you shared with them in early days and use it to remind you that you came from "humble beginnings." This is done very good-naturedly, as an invitation to return to your less bodacious days and ways.

8. *The character assassin:* This person attempts to reduce your confidence by criticizing your overall worthiness and emotional stability. You will hear expressions such as, "There you go again" or "Don't you think you're overreacting or being just a little bit paranoid?" or "You always. . ." or "Is it that time of the month already?"

9. *The threatener:* This is the person who threatens consequences that are out of proportion to merely speaking your mind: "If you ever say that again, you will be sorry." It's hard

enough to gather the courage to speak your mind, take a stand, and establish standards when your expectations are reasonable. When someone overreacts to your message in a threatening way, don't take the warnings personally, but do take note. Write it down, word for word.

In the best situations, most take-a-stand conversations are uncomfortable for both parties. You're uneasy having to express a touchy subject. And your audience (whether it's one-on-one or an entire team) isn't enjoying the process any more than you are. In a workplace setting, it's appropriate to create as safe a space as possible to share your difficult information, where everyone involved behaves respectfully and in a dignified way. Your goal is not to shame anyone, it's to achieve a business result that you desire. And your audience's role is to listen and ask respectful questions. Ideally, at the end of the encounter both parties walk away with a better understanding of how to improve performance.

If you start feeling your tension escalate because your audience has taken on any one of the roles I've just outlined, you'll know that it's just strategy. Detach your emotions from the escalated tension, tell the person that you feel you have expressed your position as clearly as possible, and end the discussion. Don't try to look for satisfaction when the person you're talking to is behaving in any of these nine ways. But if you feel that you need to, follow up with a memo or e-mail outlining your points one final time. Writing it out is not to drive your points into the ground. It documents your expectations in a clear-headed, unemotional way, and it creates an official record that you've expressed your expectations in unambiguous terms. Print a copy of your memo or e-mail.

The Notes You Take Could Save Your Career

Remember the telephone game you played as a child? A message was started at one point in a circle of friends, but it was completely changed by the time it finished the circle. And you learned that lesson as a child, when life was simple and you didn't have a lot on your mind. This was before balancing your checkbook, learning a new software program, dealing with touchy subjects with your in-laws, and comparing bids from a variety of vendors were all competing for your attention.

In the Now Economy it's even more difficult to remember who said what to whom, where, and when. It's hard to remember exactly what you said yourself, much less remember what someone said to you. Our attention is so fragmented, drawn in so many different directions, and the added interruptions of our busy days make it almost impossible to keep track accurately. A secure workplace journal, or file, is the best record you can keep of what is said, when, and what the final outcome is. Such files are important not only in keeping up with day-to-day details but also in keeping a record of possible legal issues, such as recurring incidences of harassment or a possible dispute.

A Few Short Words About the Short B-Word

The hardest part about taking a stand for what you believe in is the worry that people will stop liking you. By putting a stake in the ground, you are essentially telling your associates that what they have been doing is wrong. And if you effectively change the process, you will win. And by winning, you will have beaten them. It takes a lot of bodaciousness to be comfortable with the notion of competition, especially when the loser is someone you work with every day. In her book, *The Princessa, Machiavelli for Women*, Harriet Rubin writes,

> Most women cannot win. Not because a woman cannot fight strategically. But because no one wants her to win, and often neither does she. Both she and her opponents see to it that she fails. She herself may become consumed with guilt if she wins—guilt for having created another's loss. Men hate losing to a woman; this can prompt a counterattack. And to another woman, a triumphant woman is a lifelong threat.

To good girls and bodacious women alike, it's not pleasant to be perceived as threatening, not nice. We're socially encoded to be accommodating, to be havens of comfort and security. If our agenda means putting someone out, we often choose to take ourselves out.

When my call center associate told me that a few of the reps didn't like me, I imagined that I might have been called the B-word every now and then. When you think about it, the very behaviors that make women successful in the corporate world cause women to be labeled "bitch." Part of expanding your bodacious boundaries entails pushing back on other people's territory. You could do it as nicely and as well-intentioned as possible, but if your ambition conflicts with someone else's (which it's bound to now and then), you can count on having that word applied to you. Most achievement-oriented women have. You will be in good company. But don't let the concern about being called a bitch keep you from behaving bodaciously.

Take Charge of Your Financial Future

Sure, the New Economy seemed to crank out young millionaires like the candy production line on *I Love Lucy*. But those famous stock option windfalls were rare. For most of America, it was just another reason to feel as if you missed yet another opportunity boat. Well, you didn't.

There is one lasting lesson we can all take away from the New Economy: We're responsible not only for our careers but also for our financial security. It's not too late to get started. But it's not too soon either.

✳ **ASSUME YOU WILL HAVE TO DO MORE THAN EARN A SALARY, SAVE, AND DRAW SOCIAL SECURITY.** Simple passbook savings, combined with Social Security, will not help you build a nest egg that will help you retire in comfort and security. Your financial future depends on the active and creative role you take today in managing your money.

✳ **GET EXPERT HELP.** Books, magazines, and Web sites are available to give you basic principles and ideas for making early retirement a reality. And that's great if you enjoy independent study. For the rest of us, there are professionals who have dedicated their careers to understanding financial management. Good financial planners more than pay for themselves. They'll help you understand your dreams in financial terms and help you design a plan to reach those dreams. Select your financial planner carefully. Make sure she or he doesn't draw commission on investment vehicles that will be presented to you.

✳ **START INVESTING NOW.** Use your money to make money. That's one secret of wealthy people all over the world, and in the Now Economy it's possible for almost everyone. There are many investment choices: 401(k) accounts, IRA accounts, pension funds, mutual funds, stocks, bonds, certificates of deposit, money market accounts, saving accounts, gold or precious metals, real estate, even venture capital. Assess your risk tolerance and get involved only in investment options that allow you to sleep at night.

✳ **LEARN HOW THE STOCK MARKET WORKS.** For some the very thought of learning about the stock market makes them want to forget the whole idea of retiring. "I'll just work all my life, until I die, rather than get that pain in my stomach like I did with fifth grade word problems." But it's not as daunting as it seems. Get an easy-to-understand book on how to invest in stocks, how analysts evaluate them, and the market's typical reactions or behavior. Watch financial news programs to gain confidence and further your knowledge.

> ✳ **KEEP IT SIMPLE.** You can always get more sophisticated as you gain experience and if you want to be more daring. The more you know what's really happening with your money and the more you're involved, the more confident you'll become.

Down With Up-Talk and Other Bodacious Checkpoints

Career Year One is the last year you're allowed to play the ingenue. This is actually an excellent grace period of transition between your college days and full adulthood. This is the time when your wardrobe transitions from college to career, and this is the time to start modeling the behaviors you admire in bodacious women further up the ranks. You'll notice distinct behavior differences between those with clout and command and those without.

✳ *Bodacious women don't end every sentence with a question mark?* You know those women who can't even tell you they're going to sharpen a pencil without turning the simple statement into a question? This habit makes them sound like they're uncertain of their facts and opinions? I wouldn't feel comfortable putting them in charge of a strategically important project? I probably wouldn't even trust them to competently answer the most basic questions about the business? Would you?

✳ *Bodacious women use language to open doors, not close them.* They don't use trendy expressions such as "I was like . . .," or "Hello?" or "Whatever," unless it's done sparingly, for effect. They also don't use the word "sucks." Although it's commonly used today, it was originally a very graphic obscenity. And it's just as jarring to many ears as the f-word.

✳ *Bodacious women control the vocabulary.* To you, a project might be "an investment." To a more negative person, the same project might be "in the hole." To someone else, a person might be "broke." To you, it could just be a "temporary cash flow problem." One of you will prevail regarding the words and the tone used to describe a situation. Drive the vocabulary toward positive, optimistic, and sensible language.

* *Bodacious women keep their hands out of their hair.* And they don't scratch or fidget with their pens while talking. Nervous gestures send the signal that you're not certain of your own opinions or are feeling intimidated or nervous.

* *Bodacious women don't overexplain.* Katharine Hepburn once said, "Never complain, never explain." Katharine Hepburn is an exemplar of bodaciousness, someone we can all aspire to being like. But I don't know anyone who can get through life without complaining just a little bit now and then, or certainly without having to explain something every once in a while. But generally, women tend to overexplain. We put ourselves on the defensive by constantly feeling as though we must account for where we are, why we're there, what we're thinking, and how we arrived to that conclusion. You owe the world results, not an explanation.

* *Bodacious women act as though they already have the power of the next step up.* Fashion experts advise you to dress for the job you want to have. Given the casual workplace environment of the Now Economy, that's not always so easy to do. But you can act with the confidence of the positional power that you want to have. Work with as much confidence and autonomy as you can. Relate to those higher up the organizational chart as you would if you were their peer. This is the power of positioning.

* *Bodacious women inspire others to achieve.* You can win the battle by shedding blood, or you can win by sharing your message and vision. This second approach is a true Now Economy technique and ideal for women in leadership roles.

The more typically male approach—domination, command-and-control, my way or the highway—is passé and destructive. This is the way you get ex-employees rather than devoted followers.

* *Bodacious women notice achievements and give positive feedback.* The old management model said, "If you don't hear from me, you'll know I'm satisfied." But in the highly creative, high-stakes atmosphere of Now Economy business, your coworkers—even those higher up the hierarchy than you—want to know that you recognize and appreciate their efforts.

When Someone Takes a Stand With You

As difficult as it is to be on the giving end, it's also uncomfortable being on the receiving end of a correction or boundary being established. Most of us hate the idea that we have hurt someone or caused offense. So it's natural to be upset when someone is upset with us.

You can't control the vehemence of their feelings, but you can influence the atmosphere of the confrontation or conflict. Make people feel as though they are safe to express the pain, that it won't come back to haunt them later, and that you sincerely care about their well-being.

* If the conflict happens in a public setting, quietly guide the person into a private area such as your office or conference room. Close the door and give him or her your complete attention. So much of the aftermath of any confrontation is the feeling of embarrassment for getting emotional in front of others. The person who is upset with you may later be grateful for your consideration, even if he or she doesn't show it right then and there.

* Give the person the floor. Try not to interrupt while the person is speaking, even if you're tempted to correct a

detail. Let him or her vent. Stop the conversation only if it gets personal or loses focus.

* Don't allow outside interruptions. Switch your phone to voice mail. Tell whoever knocks on your door that you will talk to them later. This moment—as well as your attention—is reserved for the person in the room.

* Keep the conversation going until you understand the person's complaint. Your job is to understand the situation from the complainer's perspective. This doesn't mean you must agree with him or her. But you must at least see it through his or her eyes. If you really can't "get it," or if the conversation gets more and more confusing, tell the person that you want to understand and that you need some time to think over what has been said. Offer to schedule another appointment in a day or two to regroup and talk things over again. By that time the conversation won't be so emotionally charged, the person will have felt heard, and you might be able to come to a clearer understanding.

* Know exactly what will satisfy the complainer. Is it a change of behavior on your part? Is it a transfer to another department? Is it a promotion? Is it an apology from you or someone else? If you can give that person what he or she wants, without significant cost to you, great! Do it. If you can't, know that by listening you've at least given them something significant—respect.

* Apologize sincerely and without "buts." If you're sorry, say so without trying to wriggle off any hooks of responsibility. To hear, "Look, I'm really sorry, but . . ." is very unsatisfactory for the person and unbodacious of you. If you deserve to take responsibility, take responsibility, even if it means taking it on the chin. You will cultivate more respect and loyalty in the long run.

Culture Shock

Taking a stand is one of the most bodacious actions you can take. By simply saying, "This is how I want it to be," you are creating a culture shift in your life that will ripple beyond your immediate goal of making a difference in simply that one area.

You will be turning on a mechanism within your own spirit that will continue to take a stand on your behalf more often, more easily, and more gracefully with added practice.

You will be changing your immediate environment from one of neglect or disrespect to one of respect, achievement, pride, and an enduring sense of self-worth that prevails no matter what the circumstance might be.

You will be changing your friends and associates. Some people will change themselves, inspired by your example. Others will simply disappear from the scene as you both realize that the conditions have changed and your acquaintance is no longer mutually beneficial. And you will be attracting new, more powerful, more self-actualized, more bodacious new relationships.

Your conversations will change. You won't be focusing so much on problems, complaints, and unresolvable situations. You will be talking about innovations, ambition, possibilities, ideas, and ideals. These are what the Now Economy is made of!

This is a time of shift and change. And to use the Now Economy as a portal through which to step into a bigger, bolder, more authentic version of herself, the Bodacious Woman needs to surround herself with friends, family, and coworkers who support her vision, respect her boundaries, and have the courage and sense of adventure to take their own journey of bodacious self-discovery.

Bodacious Women Thrive on Shift and Change

WELCOME to the wilderness! You might as well enjoy it because you're going to be here for a long time. The key is to accept the fact that life in the Now Economy will be confusing, surprising, and unfamiliar. Will you worry and obsess about things that can go wrong? Or will you find the new vistas thrilling, knowing full well there will be hazards as well as rewards for bodaciously venturing forth?

There's a reason why this chapter title includes *shift* along with *change*. I'm hoping to encourage you to focus on the uncertainty of the shifting times as a period of benefit, just as much as the end results we are waiting for. It's human nature to focus on the end result: the actual change itself once the long shifting process is over. But it's in the *process* where the good stuff happens: growth, self-discovery, humor, amazement, and creativity. It takes a lot of nerve and spirit to thrive in the shift stage. And that's where you'll find many bodacious women, relishing the actual process. Which is a good thing because in the Now Economy I don't see very many processes culminating into any definitive finalities. This is a time of continual process. Having a good time yet?

Maybe not yet. The shift stage for you could be full of pain and fear. Maybe a marriage is suffering. Maybe you're afraid that the next layoff will include you. Maybe you're worried that you won't be able to keep up with the ongoing learning that's necessary just to stay current with developments in your profession. Maybe you're afraid that once you've journeyed through the shift process, your loved ones won't like who you've become. Or worse, maybe *you* won't like who you've become.

This is what William Bridges, author of *Transitions* and *Managing Transitions*, calls the "emotional wilderness," the feeling of fear, knowing that you're inextricably along for the Now Economy ride, without any clear idea of what the final outcome will be and very concerned that you may lose something precious in exchange for your evolution. All those are very natural concerns. The bodacious principles give you the guidance and inspiration you will need to actively design and achieve the high-performance life you know you're capable of. It's up to you to keep designing and then redesigning the next iterations of who you want to be: Now Economy You Version 2.0, Version 3.0, and so on.

Let me forewarn you: In the shift process you will go through some major culture shocks and climate changes. With every alteration in your life that you create, or any alteration that is made for you (no matter how bodacious you are, some events will be out of your hands), the shift may make you feel alien to your new circumstances, even the ones you actively choose and design. Don't worry, you'll grow into them.

Change Is Inevitable; Growth Is Optional

At AOL, my entire career was about rapid shift and change. For the first seven years, it was all in the call center. I was promoted from customer service rep to trainer to training manager and then to call center manager. Though always shifting and changing itself to serve customers, the call center had some familiarities. I knew the staff, I knew the rhythms of the day, and I knew the soundtrack of the call center. The first seven years of my career were set against the steady buzz of hundreds of voices answering thousands of calls every day: "Thank you for calling America Online. My name is _____. How may I help you?"

But soon other areas of my life—namely one last-ditch effort to save my marriage after a year's separation and maybe even start thinking about having a family—demanded that I make a major change at AOL. With the dedication and hours AOL demanded, I worried that I wasn't giving my husband the time and attention he needed to feel that I was recommitted to the marriage. A shift had happened in my life. And I needed to invest the energies I had dedicated to AOL into reviving my marriage, if I could. And for AOL's sake, I knew what kind of effect that distraction would have on my work. I didn't want to mar my performance record, and I knew that AOL needed a fully dedicated manager to oversee the growth we were still experiencing.

I considered leaving AOL altogether. But that would have been too drastic a step. I loved the company, and it was one place in my life where I could count on feeling safe, confident, and competent. I was respected, and I was earning every bit of that respect. Despite its high-pressure environment, AOL was the only place where I could relax and be my best self. I didn't want to give that up.

So I started looking around the company to see where else I might be able to offer value. When I thought about AOL's culture and our increasing belief that managers would have a huge impact on how well we were going to grow, I knew I could help the company in directing and influencing this group of contributors. It's amazing to realize that even as recently as 1995, we had no formal management training program. We were all so busy just getting the day-to-day work done that we were neglecting the ongoing development needs of the very people who were pivotal in getting results.

Setting my sites on switching over to corporate human resources, I thought I could have a greater impact throughout the organization, instead of just the call center, and maybe remove myself from the pressure-cooker atmosphere that the call center represented. Instead of ten- to twelve-hour days, maybe I could reduce it to eight or nine and get home to my husband at a decent time.

I didn't wait until I saw a job posting. I took the initiative and contacted the brand new vice president of human resources directly. He and I knew each other only slightly through some work we had done together on a couple of call center issues. Mostly I represented to him a line manager with five years of training experience already under my belt, plus an extensive history with the company. Because he was commissioned with developing a full-fledged human resources group, I thought maybe he could use someone with my background and understanding of how the company works. Additionally, he respected the fact that my heart was really into building the company through people.

Although I was motivated to make a change for personal reasons, I emphasized only my desire to help build the company from the inside out and my desire to develop management with the skills AOL needed quickly. I didn't want him to know about my personal life, partly because it wasn't his concern but also because I felt like it was a part of my life where I was failing. Also, I was concerned about my workplace image of being competent, efficient, and successful. I didn't want to plant any doubt in anyone's mind about my being able to take on a role and be completely successful at it.

He made a new job offer: corporate training manager. My career took another turn.

The Bodacious Leadership Big Six

Talk about culture shock! You know the feeling when you dive into deeper water, and there's an invisible but unmistakable line where you pass from warmth into significantly cooler water? In one instant I passed through one level where I was managing an operation of 250 people, seven days a week, and serving hundreds of thousands of customers to being what *Fast Company* magazine calls a Unit of One. In my old life I was surrounded by the buzz, the call center energy, people always walking past my door, the ongoing noises of the call center. The day I packed up my things and files and moved to the building next door, I went from that buzz to a cottony silence. I remember going down a carpeted hallway, carrying my box of belongings, and passing office after office after office after office. And I could hear nothing. It was so quiet! Where was everybody?

I thought I was on the track to gearing down, having children, becoming a stay-at-home mom, a wife in a functional if not joyful marriage. We even bought a five-bedroom house in the suburbs. In time I'd have a minivan to go with it. However, within a couple of years my marriage would be over for good. Eventually, one of my first duties would be to launch AOL's first formal manager training program and learn how I could apply to my own life—how any woman could apply to her bodacious life of shift and change—the same attributes and behaviors AOL required from its leadership staff to grow into its big vision.

But for now my main task was to settle into this new role and create training that would help develop the people we needed to grow, and fast. In other words, I was assigned to design a process to help AOL and its employees thrive in our rapidly shifting business environment and then help them understand it. Eventually that included capturing AOL's "valued work behaviors," the behaviors we identified as crucial to the company's immediate success. I realize now that these behaviors, especially the ones for our top organizational leaders, provided a great blueprint for leading change in myself, the kind of change that enables bodacious living in the Now Economy. I borrowed these behaviors and modified them for the Unit of One called myself.

VALUED BEHAVIOR 1: DEFINE YOUR STRATEGY

You're able to determine the strategies that support your objectives. AOL's objectives included sustainable growth, profitability, and dominant share. I suspect that your objectives may be different. Still, many of the strategies may apply:

* You develop an understanding of your strengths and weaknesses, especially in the context of the opposing forces of your change objective.

* You maintain relationship networks outside your immediate circle of close contacts.

* You share your discoveries and inspiration with others who could benefit themselves and support you in reaching your change objective.

* You stay current on key trends that could affect your change objective.

* You balance short-term benefits with long-term objectives when choosing among options.

* You take advantage of unexpected opportunities.

What you don't do: You don't jump to conclusions, you don't focus all your attention on internal situations to the exclusion of understanding external environments, you don't fail to share critical information with others, and you don't fail to integrate your change objective with all other areas of your life, career, or business.

VALUED BEHAVIOR 2: BUILD YOUR OPERATING PLAN

You're able to develop and put into action an operating plan, complete with objectives and measurements, that supports the business strategy and integrates the change project into the rest of your "organization."

* You recruit the right people at the right time to help support your objectives.

* You anticipate disruptions and develop contingency plans.

* You manage risk.

* You continue to review your plan to make sure your goals are still appropriate to changing conditions.

* You remain flexible and integrate changing priorities as the environment changes.

* You establish milestones and ways to measure your progress.

* You design realistic time and money budgets.

What you don't do: You don't fail to identify definite and measurable objectives, you don't fail to anticipate negative consequences of your plan, you don't fail to properly budget the amount of time you dedicate to your various priorities, and you don't operate in a continual crisis mode, putting unnecessary and unpleasant pressure on yourself and others.

VALUED BEHAVIOR 3: CREATE CAPABILITY

You are constantly learning new ways to realize your change objective.

* You consistently improve your performance in important areas, such as productivity, quality, timeliness, and cost.

* You don't "buy retail" if you can avoid it. You find creative ways and resources for getting the help and equipment you need to support your project.

* You reassess the overall structure of your plan every now and then to make sure it's current.

* You use the technology and tools that are available to you to make the job easier.

What you don't do: You don't build your plan based on emotional reactions or personalities of the people involved, you don't try to make your objective happen without the people and other support it needs, you don't change the plan unnecessarily or in a desperate frame of mind, you don't go outside for support when you should stay inside, and you don't stay inside when you should go outside.

VALUED BEHAVIOR 4: BUILD COMMITMENT

Make sure the people you've gathered to help implement your change plan are committed to following through.

* You use a variety of messages to cultivate the commitment (such as reason, personal gain, and opportunity for exposure).

* You know and include the personal motivations of each team member when designing the plan.

* You challenge your supporters to achieve new personal bests, reminding them that this is a growth opportunity for everyone involved.

* You acknowledge your own mistakes and missteps.

* You keep your team informed of all developments that pertain to them.

* You give credit where credit's due.

What you don't do: You don't take all the credit, you don't publicly chastise team members, you don't play favorites, and you don't micromanage, but you don't practice a laissez-faire management style either.

VALUED BEHAVIOR 5: DEMONSTRATE COURAGE

You make tough decisions and own the outcome of your actions.

* You know in advance when a tough decision is looming on the horizon, and you gather as much information as possible to prepare in advance.

* You provide as much information as you can to everyone affected by the situation and by the decisions you make.

* You give others the opportunity to learn from your mistakes.

What you don't do: You don't back off from difficult decisions, you don't lay blame on others, you don't make hard decisions without consulting a few people for advice, you don't consult with too many people for advice, and you don't rely on just your intuition for important decisions.

VALUED BEHAVIOR 6: MAINTAIN COMPOSURE
You respond to high-pressure situations calmly and confidently.

* You create an optimistic environment that prevails even in emergencies.

* You calmly handle crises in a way that builds relationships.

* You remember to express genuine concern for your team members, knowing that they're trying to cope with their own anxieties while working to help you meet your change objective.

What you don't do: You don't lose your temper, you don't squelch opposing opinions, you don't freeze in the face of an emergency, and you don't dwell on past disagreements or failures of your team members.

Launch the Change Reaction
Working on these valued behaviors was one of my most important projects while at AOL, largely because of the hectic workplace environment and largely because my own life hadn't stopped morphing wildly from being a young married woman, to being separated, to being reconciled, to being freshly resolved to end a marriage that was doomed, to adjusting to my new identity and a return to my maiden name and all that that symbolized: the feeling of failure, the refreshed self-esteem, and the renewed hope that I could build a new life of meaning and purpose as a single person again.

Between 1994 and 1997, AOL mushroomed from 400 employees to 7,500, and we were tasked to hire more. Revenues went from $100 million to $2 billion. We had gone from a small, domestic company sharing an office building to a multinational with more than twelve major locations throughout the world.

We had a lot to do! Without the guiding principles of the valued behaviors we could have been swamped by panic or chaos. We could have focused on the wrong change objectives, choosing to put out brightly burning fires that were ultimately inconsequential instead of focusing on the larger mission. This was the height of what I call AOL adrenaline. It was exciting, it was explosive. It could have been hair-trigger, but it wasn't because we consistently knew what we were about, what our values were, and what the ultimate goal was.

I was learning how to implement change in a living case study that would beat all case studies. Here's what I learned.

CREATE CHANGE IN HALF-STEPS

At AOL we were creating change in giant strides, but in my personal life I discovered that the best way was in half-steps. Chic Thompson, creativity consultant and author of *What a Great Idea!*, says that the ideas that stand the best chance of success are the ones only fifteen minutes ahead of their time. So it is with personal change. The half-steps create changes that stick. When we lose weight gradually, we stand a better chance of keeping it off. When we give ourselves half-step milestones for a huge revolution in our lives, we can stop, acknowledge the progress, congratulate ourselves for the improvement, and then step up to the next level.

Half-steps also allow you to test whether the progress is giving you the desired results. Rock climbers know that it's important to always keep three points of contact with the rock (two feet and one hand or two hands and one foot) while reaching forward or reaching up. That way, they can make sure their next foothold or handhold is secure before committing themselves to it. The same goes for any significant life change. I could have decided to leave AOL in favor of saving a marriage that ultimately should not and could not have been saved anyway. And I considered it. But that giant stride would have been in conflict with my personal desire to be part of this exciting adventure of building a company that would change the way the world communicates. The half-step allowed me to stay part of this adventure while conserving my time and energy to nurture my marriage.

LEAD WITH YOUR VALUE

You don't know what you don't know. As you research your options, look beneath the apparent. The alchemy of your passions combined with external needs may create an opportunity for you that hadn't existed before you started your research. I didn't know the human resources vice president was considering including a corporate training manager on his team when I started looking around AOL for alternatives to my high-pressure call center manager position.

I just believed I could make a difference that way and had what it took to do it. And the new vice president saw that. He recognized my package of skills, dedication, and experiences and knew he could leverage them in a way that would benefit the entire company, not just the call center. And so he asked me to go corporate.

EXPECT SOME INITIAL DISCOMFORT

Not only did I experience an environmental culture shock, all alone in my quiet office, but I had to create the job with measurable skills and objectives. Fortunately, in all of my previous positions I was essentially creating it from scratch. Still, I'd never built a training function for an entire company. My ability to produce would be seen by everyone in the company, and that number was constantly growing.

Shift and change. Remember, it comes with the territory. And this is where the emotional wilderness that William Bridges talks about in *Managing Transitions* is especially evident. There's the pain of loss. As Bridges writes, "[Planners and implementers] forget that while the first task of change management is to understand the destination and how to get there, the first task of transition management is to convince people to leave home." Your own personal transition management is to convince yourself to leave home, whether "home" is a department, old habits, or a home life that has become toxic to you.

There's the pain of uncertainty. Old weaknesses and insecurities that you managed to efficiently camouflage in the old systems suddenly make themselves obvious again. You might even get sick. The stress of change can lower your immunity and cause you to catch the flu, a cold, or a case of hives. You may temporarily feel like a mess.

MAKE CHANGE FUN

Steve Case is a master at keeping up the spirits of AOL employees. No occasion is too small for a party. In the earliest, cash-strapped days, we celebrated on Friday afternoons with beer bashes. He believes in fostering a spirit of community and shared every milestone in an all-hands meeting, followed by an increasingly lavish and ever more fun party. I know there have been plenty of fabulous parties since, but the one I remember most fondly was the one where Steve bit off more than he probably expected to chew.

It was in March 1995 and we were celebrating reaching 2 million members. By this time, AOL parties had gone big time, and the company wisely had its parties off-site, with rented buses to keep AOL revelers away from their car keys. And wow, could we revel! I'm not much of a drinker, but everyone else was. So I knew I could dance on a table with only a few noticing it or remembering it the next day. So I did!

Steve was strutting around wearing a fantastic black leather bomber jacket with "AOL" embroidered in gold on the back. People came up to him all afternoon telling him how much they loved it. Either he got one compliment too many or one beer too many, because at the climax of the party he went up to a microphone and said, "Since you all like my jacket so much, here's a challenge for you: If we reach 5 million members by this time next year, everyone will get a jacket of their own!"

The room exploded with cheers. Everyone loved it. We rededicated our focus to increasing the membership from 2 million to 5 million in just twelve months. And we did it! And Steve came up with the goods, even to the point of returning the first shipment of jackets because they weren't good enough (they had vinyl arms instead of leather).

Shared fun is as much a galvanizing force as shared work and shared focus. There's a lot of leverage in memories of laughter and good times. That's a resource to be cherished. And Steve was a hero twice: once for making such a bodacious offer and again a year later for not only keeping his word but demonstrating through his actions that he believed we deserved the best.

TAKE A STEP DOWN WHEN IT'S STRATEGIC FOR YOUR LONG-TERM OBJECTIVES

In career management circles, there's a lot of talk about the time-honored career ladder (where you go up and down) transforming into a career lattice (where you also move sideways as a way of progressing in your life's work). In her speeches and workshops, Martha has added a new dimension to this model: the career *landscape*. In the Now Economy, you're no longer limited to two-dimensional movement. You can move all around the landscape: up, down, sideways, way over there, way over here, up another silo, down a different wall, even underground if it's a strategically bodacious move.

And you can even move down to shoot back up to a higher level. This is not a loss of stature; this is a bodacious shift in position. But it makes sense only if you're doing it strategically and other people are in on the plan. In AOL's earliest days Steve Case took a step down from head honcho to vice honcho because the company was about to go public. And senior leadership agreed that initially institutional investors probably wouldn't have faith in a company led by someone so young. So he took a demotion to position the company's leadership as being experienced and compellingly investment worthy. And once AOL's Wall Street objectives were met and the company proved its performance potential to investors, young Steve Case resumed his title and role.

One female executive at another Fortune 500 company in Northern Virginia took a nine-step demotion as a strategic move to ultimately gain access to the executive suite. She needed to get more line management experience before she could continue moving up. Her investment paid off. She retired as senior vice president of human resources.

This shift can understandably make you nervous. But if it's strategic, it's bodacious. So go for it!

GET OUTSIDE PERSPECTIVE WHENEVER YOU CAN

You have no idea how good you really are until you leave your fishbowl. When we're sealed up in our own environment, working hard and focusing on the tasks immediately in front of us, we lose perspective. It's easy to fall into the trap of self-criticism without any real sense of how we compare to external colleagues. Get out and about! You may discover that you are further ahead than you thought you were.

That came home to me loud and clear the first year AOL was invited to make a presentation to the Ken Blanchard Companies' annual client conference. This is a high-profile event in which Blanchard's preferred clients gather, compare their experiences and results, and learn from one another. I considered it an honor and opportunity to not only attend but also to be invited to give a presentation.

I wanted to do something that would blow their socks off. Something that was really motivating, fun, energetic, useful to show off AOL and show off our training. I assembled some rock music, an MTV-like company video, and a PowerPoint presentation that told the story of our hypergrowth and how Blanchard helped get us through the adventure. This was one bodacious program, I thought.

When it was show time my hands were clammy, my heart was pounding, and my suit was bright blue. The room was packed, the lights dimmed, so it was on with the show! The response was amazing. Lots of wide eyes, lots of smiles, and lots of applause. The first time I ever met Marjorie Blanchard, Ken's wife, was when she shot up and gave me a big hug when it was all over. I found out later that the presentation scored the highest among all the ones that year.

At that moment I began to realize how extraordinary my AOL career was and what a powerful position I had developed for myself. At that moment I started to realize my growing dissatisfaction with not getting the full credit I felt I deserved at work. I wouldn't have completely appreciated that fact if I was back in Northern Virginia focusing on the next training rollout.

A few days later, at the conference's closing dinner, I received an unexpected award. As Ken congratulated me, he asked, "So, when are you going to come work with us?" Here I was in front of 200 clapping people getting a job offer from one of the country's most highly respected thought leaders. Then, a few weeks after I returned, I got a voice mail. "Hi Mary. A colleague of mine saw you at the Blanchard client conference. I'm with a company looking for an organizational development director and wanted to know if you're available." Talk about getting a perspective!

Organizational development director—precisely the AOL position for which I was passed over for not being strategic enough.

But I took a pass on both opportunities. My personal strategy took a different direction: grad school.

LEVERAGE YOUR CHOICES

There will be changes and choices in your life that go way beyond half-steps. These are life-changing, revolutionary decisions. When those opportunities come along, make the most self-affirming choice that's available to you and then give it all you've got to make that choice successful.

As I've said before, transitions for me tend to happen in stereo. One channel of change always seems to support the other channel of change, if only to give me the confidence and sense of self I need at the moment to make the hard decisions.

At that point in my life, the first choice was to end my marriage. I had invested almost two and a half years of honest and earnest effort into the reconciliation of this unhealthy relationship. While my frantic parents watched and worried, I had walked back into a marriage that offered only pain and emotional damage, and I had given it my best shot.

But this wasn't going to be the frightened escape that I made a couple of years earlier. This time I would coolly make the arrangements I needed to make to leave the marriage safely. One morning after he left for work, I loaded my car with all my clothes and a few personal belongings. I had already lined up a place to stay for a few nights until I found something more permanent. And I arranged with a friend to meet me outside our counselor's office that night after our appointment was over.

It was at the counselor's office that I broke the news to my husband. Then, with him still sitting in his chair, I got up, walked out, and left him and that life behind me forever.

The next step was to decide what to do about my career. I'd already asked my boss why I wasn't being fully recognized for my abilities. Now that was a dead-end road. He chose to fill a position with someone else. I knew I wanted to do the same kind of work of helping to build the people side of organizations. I also wanted more challenge. If I couldn't find that at AOL, I already knew other organizations would be more than happy to have me on board. But even though I knew I could jump right into a new position at another company, I wanted to learn even more about the profession first. So I decided that the next step was grad school.

But which grad school, where, and when? I knew a few people with such degrees, so I thought I'd start by asking them about their schools. I checked out Web sites and called program offices for information. Another task was to decide what I preferred as a school experience. Did I want something local? Was I after a more theoretical slant or an application perspective? What was the cost? I also needed to know the prerequisite and application requirements. Did I have to take any kind of entrance exam? Write a paper?

Get recommendations? Have a faculty interview? When was the deadline? All of these were specific tactics to make this giant stride a reality.

I narrowed my choices to two schools based on my desire for a highly ranked program that was application oriented and packaged in a highly interactive learning environment. Both required the Graduate Record Examination (GRE), so I set out to find where I could take it and what it involved. What I found was that to make my application deadlines I had to take the exam in about two weeks! So I signed up and crammed until test day. I postponed the rest of my life while preparing for that exam, taking practice tests again and again.

My results were okay but not outstanding. Fortunately, the applications gave me other opportunities to persuade the schools to accept me; one was the letters of recommendation.

And here's where I got bodacious. The schools wanted two letters, and I gave them four. And I pulled out the big guns. I asked Ken Blanchard and Steve Case to sign letters of endorsement, which they both did. I made it as easy as possible for them by composing a draft for them to start from and modify. I remember getting an e-mail from Steve's assistant telling me it was ready. I rushed upstairs to pick the letter up from his assistant. Steve was in his office, so I nervously knocked on his door and peeked in to thank him. He looked up and smiled. "Thanks for the letter, Steve. This is really going to neutralize my GRE scores!" He laughed and wished me the best of luck. And I walked away with gold in my hand.

But the most difficult challenge was posed by my first-choice school, Pepperdine University in California. Its application package included an extremely lengthy questionnaire that probed deeply into my emotional life, stability, and self-knowledge. I can understand their concern: Accepting a student is an investment for them, too, and they want to be as certain as they can be that the whole experience will be successful. But this, I thought, could be a showstopper for me. Forget the GREs, forget the to-die-for letters of recommendation. I was in the middle of one of life's major crises: a separation leading to divorce. They may decide to pass me up, reasoning that I would need more time to heal before taking on the heavy load of their curriculum. But I played it as honestly and proactively as I knew how. I told them the status of my marriage, where I was in the process, and the support I was receiving from my family, friends, and employer to pursue this degree.

On May 4, 1998, I came home to my apartment and found a letter with the return address of Pepperdine. Inside the letter read, "Dear Mary: On behalf of the faculty and staff of Pepperdine University George L. Graziadio School of Business and Management, please accept our congratulations on your acceptance into the Masters of Science in Organizational Development (MSOD) Program."

I was in!

But there was still one more change yet to come.

The Choice Is Always Yours

Within a month of receiving my acceptance letter was the day I forgot my pants. Remember that one? It became very clear to me then that I was still emotionally overextended, and I needed to take care of myself, especially if I was going to have enough time and energy for grad school.

I wasn't ready to leave AOL as I was still finalizing my divorce agreement, and the thought of starting a whole new job while starting grad school didn't make much sense. But something had to give, so I asked whether I could go part-time. Part-time. That's an oxymoron at a fast-paced, highly demanding company like AOL, but I went for it anyway. AOL didn't want to see me leave, so they created a training instructor position for me that required giving up my manager role. I chose to take a step down to get the space I needed. Over the next few months I honestly tried to make the arrangement work, but even the partial load was almost 40 hours a week, and still way more than I wanted. The time had come to leave the company I loved so much.

Not long after that day, I walked into my boss's office and nervously gave him the news that I wanted to reduce my hours yet again. This time to zero.

"Oh, you'll be back in six months," my boss said, but this time it was goodbye.

The decision was made. And I wasn't going to unmake it. It was time to see what the big, wide world had for me. It was hard to imagine a working world outside the context of AOL, but at 33 it wasn't too late for me to discover it. Grad school felt like the obvious transition step.

But before I quit AOL I understood at least one thing politically and personally: Ending well was vitally important for my relationships and for me. It doesn't do you or others much good to take ten years of your life and make your last official interaction full of resentment. Not everything had to be perfect to see all the amazing, positive experiences AOL gave me. I knew that my last days at AOL would be what I made them, so I decided to activate my personal power by bringing closure my own way. I gave myself the experience of making a difference within the AOL walls one last time.

I chose my last day to be the day after I finished a series of workshops for a vice presidents' group I admired. Instead of each workshop feeling like a hassle, it felt like a last personal imprint on the organization that gave me so much. As my last week started, I made a list of people I wanted to say goodbye to. I made a point of seeing many of them before I left (at this point AOL had 12,000 employees spread out all over the United States). But because of distance and time, I knew my last day would come before I'd be able to see everyone in person. I knew that the power of e-mail we'd shared with the world was the most effective and appropriate solution.

Sitting down to write this goodbye e-mail took me back to my senior year in high school when we wrote our "last will and testament." We were so serious and so clueless! But it meant something then, and what I was about to compose meant something too. However, this time I wanted to use all I had learned and experienced to say what was most important. I sat staring at my monitor while my brain pored over memories and my heart rode the emotional waves.

Then I knew. Of all the things I could say about all the amazing things we did, what felt the most authentic and meaningful was to focus on my experience with people. Steve Case often talked about how community was at the core of the online experience, the human experience. And so I typed my last e-mail as an AOL employee, stood up, switched off my computer, slid my chair toward the desk, picked my briefcase up off the floor, turned in my badge, and went home.

I sold the minivan and replaced it with a Porsche. That's the car I later drove west to California, with my mother riding shotgun.

> FROM: Mary Foley
> DATE: 01/29/99
> SUBJECT: Thank you!
>
> Studies show that people don't usually stay long term at a company because of the money, power, or prestige. Nope, it's usually because they can work on challenging stuff and do it with some great people. That's the case with me.
>
> All of you have in some way contributed to my experience of working with great people. Each of you have given me something, be it a sincere smile, encouraging word, belief in me, sage advice, helpful feedback, role model, or direct mentorship. For that I want to say THANK YOU!
>
> I wish you all the best in your continued adventure with AOL. I'm sure there are more great things to come!

```
If you'd like to stay in touch, please
use my new screen name. . . . I'll only
be an e-mail away . . . on the "other
side."
```

The Bodacious Thrive-on-Change Six-Pack

Shift and change in the New Economy often involves changing jobs and companies. Here's my bodacious six-pack on surviving a layoff and what to do when you get a new job.

1. How to Survive a Layoff

Layoffs are a fact of life in the Now Economy. It's a terrible moment to hear that through no fault of your own, your company has decided it doesn't need you anymore. It's also terrible to survive a round of cuts, then come to work the next day and find yourself surrounded by empty desks that once belonged to people you had worked with, laughed with, and counted on. Either way, it's a sad day when layoffs are announced. Although you may not be able to prevent a layoff at your company, there are steps you can take to minimize the damage it can do to your career and self-esteem:

If You Keep Your Job

* **CONNECT YOUR POSITION WITH CORPORATE GOALS.** Know exactly how your job helps your company meet its operational and profit objectives. Be able to talk about your function in terms of business strategy. Know how the company is doing in its market, among customers, and on the stock exchange. Find ways to link your position with its performance in those areas.

* **MAKE YOURSELF INDISPENSABLE.** Make friends with key players in other departments; volunteer for cross-

functional projects; if your job is a cost center, expand your job description to include profit center activities.

* **SHOW UP.** Go to and participate in all appropriate meetings. Demonstrate through your actions and contributions that you are passionate about the company's long-term vision.

* **DON'T FEEL GUILTY.** It's not a crime to survive a round of layoffs. But it's also common to feel survivor's guilt when you come to work and see only darkened cubicles and empty desks. Remember that it's not your fault. Don't let your feelings of responsibility sabotage your effectiveness and career. Use this as an opportunity to expand your skills and value to the company.

* **STAY IN TOUCH WITH THOSE WHO ARE LAID OFF.** These people are now out in the big wide world, making important contacts and sending their own careers in new and exciting directions. You may be able to help them in the future, but just as likely they may be able to help you in the future.

* **DECIDE WHETHER YOU WANT TO STAY.** After several months or even a year in the post-layoff environment, the company environment or mission may be so different that you feel it's no longer a good fit anymore. This is the time to remember that in the Now Economy we're all free agents, giving our valuable talent in exchange for a paycheck and meaningful career. We can choose to stay just as much as the company can choose to ask us to leave. Because it's usually easier to find the next opportunity while you're still working in the current one, try to line up the next job before you hand in your notice. And remember to leave on as positive a note as possible.

If You Get Laid Off

* **DON'T TAKE IT PERSONALLY.** You don't need self-recrimination to make you feel worse than you already do. Although companies often use the layoff process as a way to get rid of dead wood, that doesn't necessarily mean that you were fired for lack of performance. If you can look back at your time with the company and know that you performed well, at least take comfort in knowing you did everything you could have done.

* **DON'T SIGN ANYTHING RIGHT AWAY.** In the meeting where you get the bad news, they may hand you a stack of documents to digest right away and sign. Don't. Take at least twenty-four hours and, if you can, show the documents to an attorney (you can be sure they did and that any agreements will have been written in favor of the employer).

* **DON'T ACCEPT THE FIRST OFFER.** It's possible that you will be able to negotiate a more beneficial severance package, including one to two weeks' pay for each year you have worked at the company, a plan to allow your stock options to vest earlier than the original schedule, the ability to continue to use your office and phone (or voice mail), and reference letters from top management.

* **EXPLORE A CONSULTING OPTION WITH THE COMPANY.** Your position may be eliminated, but that doesn't mean the workload is. If you can redefine your job in terms of smaller projects, you may be able to renegotiate your relationship with the company. You stand to save the company money and keep a steady cash flow while you consider other options. Consulting also keeps you on good terms with the company, which may benefit you once the company starts to staff up again.

* **BE SURE TO USE COMPANY-SPONSORED OUTPLACEMENT SER-VICES.** Almost every major company layoff includes helping former employees transition to the next job by providing professional outplacement services. You can get expert help in exploring your aptitude, talents, and passions, learning interviewing techniques, and finding leads for jobs at other companies. This is a very valuable service, so use it.

* **START GOING TO REGULAR MEETINGS OF YOUR PROFESSIONAL ASSOCIATION AND OTHER BUSINESS GATHERINGS NEAR YOU.** Get out of the house as much as you can, meet new people, and explore all options and possibilities. Even consider working as a temp. Temp agencies are filling openings from basic secretary to CEO. This is a great way to expand your network of contacts, learn new skills, earn money, and keep your confidence intact.

* **THROW "PINK SLIP" PARTIES.** There are three facts of the Now Economy layoff: There's no shame in it, you're not alone, and recruiters are still desperate for your kind of talent. Put those facts together and you've got the makings of a party. Instead of slinking off in shame or embarrassment, use a company layoff as the excuse for a party bringing together in an upbeat, low-pressure, social environment your fellow layoffees and the best recruiters in your area. You won't be just helping yourself; you'll be helping others while you're at it.

* **STAY IN TOUCH WITH FORMER COWORKERS.** Many survivors feel badly that you're gone, and they'll want to know that you're okay. Here's your chance to reassure and surprise them. Now that you're in the outside world, you'll hear of job opportunities not only for yourself but for them as well. One caution, however: Survivors who have been assigned your duties may call you for

advice, information, or how-tos. Don't give away your expertise. Convert this demand for your knowledge into a paid consulting position to help your successors take on your responsibilities.

Whether you are a victim or a survivor of a layoff, it may feel like the end of a dream. But it doesn't have to be the end of hope. You can leverage the experience and come out the better for it.

---

2. How to Interview in the Now Economy

What we can often forget when we're not living bodaciously is that when you're looking for a new job you are interviewing the company as much as they are interviewing you. It's about match and exchange. Do they have what you want, and do you have what they want?

If you feel desperate for a job, you've already put yourself at a disadvantage. Everything about the company, position, and people will look a lot rosier than it probably is. You're much more vulnerable taking whatever's offered rather than assessing the situation for real, personal satisfaction. The same can happen if the company is desperate for you, which isn't unlikely given today's war for talent. It may view your abilities as greater than they are, and you may end up in a spot where it's tough for you to succeed. Or it may spin the company's situation so optimistically that it doesn't see its own problems, nor do you.

In the Now Economy you need to get an accurate picture of the company's situation to make your best decision. The bottom line: You have to think like someone investing in or buying the business as well as someone working in it. Before any interview, do your homework on the company. Check out its stock market performance if the company is public. How has it done the last few quarters? The last year? What's its stock price trend over the last few years? Does it have a track record of hitting its performance targets? Check out the company's Web site for quarterly and annual reports. Even if you can't understand the spreadsheets, read the descriptive overview. What markets is it in? What are its products or services? Who are its competitors? How does it rank against them? Does it have a track record of growth and performance? At what evolutionary stage is it: start-up, high-growth, mature, or past peak? How is the CEO portrayed? If it's a private company, still try to find what you can. Articles on the Web from the last twelve months may help you find these facts.

Come to the interview prepared with questions to ask as well as answers to give. Here are some suggestions for new questions to ask in the Now Economy and what to listen for in the responses.

✳ **WHAT'S BEEN THE COMPANY'S PERCENTAGE GROWTH THE LAST THREE TO FIVE YEARS?** Wall Street measures growth by financial numbers, typically revenues or profits. If they tell you only the customer or production growth, they may be hiding the fact that actual profits didn't increase. Do they portray company growth the same as you found in your research? If not, what is this telling you?

✳ **WHAT IMPROVEMENTS OR INNOVATIONS HAS THE COMPANY MADE IN THE PAST FEW YEARS TO REMAIN COMPETITIVE?** Listen for a proactive stance to continually change and innovate as needed in today's market, both internally and externally. Standing still is not an option to thrive in the Now Economy.

✳ **WHO ARE YOUR COMPETITORS, AND HOW DO YOU RANK AGAINST THEM?** Listen for solid company knowledge of the competition. Every company has competition, so who are they and what are they about? Besides, such information may benefit you if you want to check out opportunities at other companies.

* **WHERE DOES THE COMPANY SEE ITSELF IN THE NEXT TWO TO THREE YEARS?** How will it get there? If the company doesn't have a clear sense of direction and strategic plan for the next few years, the ones after that are even more in question. Listen for a clear vision and mission with a specific strategy to get where it wants to go. Does it make sense to you? Does it seem achievable? Did the company achieve its strategic goals the last two to three years?

* **WHAT THREE WORDS WOULD YOU USE TO DESCRIBE THE COMPANY'S CULTURE?** Just like a country's culture, every company has one, and it influences everything that happens there. Listen for a quick, positive response. That would indicate that the culture is strong and perceived positively for the company to achieve its goals. A hesitant response may indicate that the person doesn't want to share his or her immediate thoughts. The culture is the environment you'll live in if you work there. Do you like what you hear? Is it a good match for your personal style?

* **WHAT IS THE AVERAGE TENURE OF YOUR EMPLOYEES?** Listen for very short or very long periods of time. Tenures of two years or less may indicate an internal problem that isn't clear to you on the outside. Tenures of ten years or more may indicate that this is a great place to work, but they also may tip you off to internal stagnation or lack of upward mobility.

* **WHAT IS THE COMPANY'S EMPLOYEE TURNOVER RATE?** How much of this is voluntary? Listen for anything over 15 percent. Twenty percent means one out of every five people is leaving each year. What's wrong with this place? The exception might be a specific industry.

For example, front-line customer service jobs can have a turnover rate of 40 percent or more; it's just the nature of the job and hourly wage wars.

✳ **WHAT DOES THE COMPANY DO TO RETAIN EMPLOYEES?** We're talking more than benefits here; smart companies know they need more than good benefits to keep good performers longer. Listen for common benefits plus elements of a company retention strategy, such as additional benefits to help juggle other aspects of your life, a results-oriented culture, or employee development programs. Do they offer child care? A fitness center? Onsite banking? Postal service? Flex time? Telecommuting? Concierge service? Bonuses? Opinion surveys?

---

3. How to Evaluate Multiple Job Offers

This is the epitome of being in the driver's seat of your Now Economy career, which we all seem to fantasize about at one time or another: being thought of so highly that several big-hitter companies want you all at once. Numerous corporate admirers are simultaneously courting you. Your dilemma is trying to pick the best while letting the others down easy.

Don't let the flattery overcome your ability to assess and analyze. Enjoy the attention. Let it pump your ego. But don't let it take you on a ride where you ultimately don't want to go. To know what ride you do want to take, you have to consider what matters most. Here's one approach: Consider the following factors and then rank them from most to least important. Having trouble deciding which factors are most important? Pay attention to your initial gut reaction to each topic; you *will* have one, so listen and trust yourself. (Caution: Don't engage in mental "shoulds" or outside opinions. There are no right answers, just best answers for you. You're the one who has to live with the job, and you won't do well if you're going against yourself.)

After you've ranked the factors, compare each job offer against your list. Which ones match your top factors? Of those, which ones best match with the remaining factors? Often the best choice becomes clear. Remember that no company, position, or offer is perfect, so you probably won't get absolutely everything you want. You may have to trade some job security for exciting work, for example. The bodacious thing is to be fully aware of your choice, how you made it, and any tradeoffs.

* **JOB SECURITY.** That's truly an oxymoron in the Now Economy, but perhaps what you need more than anything is stability from a company. If this company is likely to be around longer than others and supplies you with needed income, then maybe this is the one to choose. (You did do your company homework, right? If not, see the sidebar "How to Interview in the Now Economy.") No company is a sure bet, but some don't demand nearly the risk tolerance that others do.

* **INTERESTING WORK.** Maybe the only thing that gets your mojo working is variety and new challenges on the job. You want to be continually stimulated, improve your skills, and expand your professional experience. In fact, you need to be passionate about your job for it to feel worthwhile.

* **CAREER GROWTH.** You want to expand your skills and abilities, and you want a company that supports your ambition. You want serious opportunities to attend training, go to conferences, and work on projects that will cause you to stretch. You also want the ability to move up or over to enhance your career.

* **MONEY.** Whether it's the status, freedom, or things you can buy (or bought and have to pay for), money is at the top of your list. THE top. You're willing to go the extra mile for the job if you're well compensated.

* **RANK.** You've risen or are aspiring to a certain organizational level and aren't willing to go lower. Above all else, title matters, even within a small organization. You want that positional power and are willing to downgrade other factors to get it.

* **ENVIRONMENT.** You've worked in some places where people didn't treat each other well and the employer set the tone. Now it's imperative to have an atmosphere where the employer shows real care for employees and people like coming to work.

* **AUTONOMY.** If you don't have some elbow room in making decisions on the job, you'll go nuts! And not decisions of whether or not to buy blue or black ink pens, but real decisions that nurture your creativity and bring out your best work (and best you).

* **PERSONAL TIME.** You are willing to work hard and do your part, but you don't want 70-hour weeks for months or years on end. Your time away from work is particularly important to you, filled with Little League games, recitals, charity work, concerts, cooking, fishing, sailing, collecting stamps, you name it. The important thing is that there's plenty of time out of the office to call your own.

* **TRAVEL.** Or lack of travel. You want to see the country or the world, and a job is your travel ticket. Or perhaps you've seen enough hotel rooms and want to stay in the same place. Either way, how much travel the job requires is a big deal, a showstopper.

* **OTHER.** There are as many factors to consider as there

are people. Fill in the blank as needed—whatever topic helps you sort out what's most important to you so you can choose the offer that best suits you.

----

4. There's Almost Always More Money: What Most Employers Don't Want You to Know When They Talk Salary

When it comes to negotiating a salary package, most American women are clueless. The good girl mode kicks in under pressure. We're afraid of looking too aggressive, ungrateful, greedy, or full of ourselves. If this new job is an opportunity we want badly, it goes against our social skills training to ask for an even better compensation and benefits package than the one originally offered to us. One woman I know took a $4,000 pay cut from the posted salary because her hirer said that although she was the most qualified for the job of all the candidates, she was too young to be making that kind of money. She knows better now.

When hiring, managers describe the salary and bene-fits package to you, they have one main objective in mind: to get the most possible talent for the least possible expense. So they're not going to volunteer the fact that they can go higher in salary or negotiate concessions in your benefits package. Here's how it works:

* **SALARY.** Well-managed companies conduct regular labor market assessments to determine whether they're paying competitive salaries. They use this information to adjust their established pay ranges for each position. Because payroll is one of the biggest expenses of running a business, they often offer the lowest salary possible to keep you satisfied.

    What they do want you to know: It's their philosophy to pay competitively. They want you to feel that your skills and abilities are valued so you will produce good work.

What they don't want you to know: How your own salary compares with the established pay range (don't assume it's within the range). Generally, if your hiring manager thinks you will be satisfied with a salary below the pay range, he or she will extend the initial offer below that spread. Remember, the employer's first offer is the *beginning* of your negotiation discussion, not the end of it.

Always ask for more than their initial offer, even if it's only $2,000 or $3,000 more. Why? You'll communicate to them that you highly value yourself and the contributions you can offer to their company. This will send the company the signal to value you as well.

Consult these Web sites for more information on salaries and ranges:

www.salary.com

www. ecomponline.com

www.dbm.com

✳ **BONUSES, COMMISSIONS, AND MERIT INCREASES.** Find out whether the company has a bonus or commission plan. Because the labor market is still in your favor, hiring managers will be willing to take the time to explain these added incentives. Every company handles these plans differently, if they have any plan installed at all. Most companies include merit increases as part of their performance review system. Find out what the review process is, how performance is measured and rewarded, and what range of increases you could expect. If there is a high demand for your profession, you should also ask for a signing bonus.

* **BENEFITS.** Benefits are like money in your pocket. Consider them carefully and in detail as you balance the entire compensation package. You can expect to get as much as another third of the value of your salary in benefits. There are the basics, such as health insurance and paid sick and vacation leave, and then a huge menu of additional support such as child care and 401(k) plans with matching contributions. But you might be able to negotiate other benefits, such as paid tuition, company car or car allowance, health club membership, or additional time off. Many of these perks often are there for the asking. Women just have a hard time asking for them.

* **MAKE THE NEGOTIATION WORK FOR YOU.** Know your worth. Don't be shy. Don't appear desperate. Don't worry about appearing greedy. Know what you want. Get the agreement in writing.

----

5. Stock Options: Explain That Again, Please

Your bodacious approach to finding the job of your dreams has landed you a golden opportunity. Part of the gold, it seems, is that the company offers stock options as a part of your compensation. You understand stock: It's a piece of a company, and most public ones trade on Wall Street, where the price of that piece constantly changes, but at least you can always look it up. But how do stock options work? You need to know these answers before you can evaluate the compensation you're being offered.

First, a few terms:

* **STOCK OPTION.** It's the opportunity to buy shares of a specified company stock at a fixed price over a set period of time.

* **GRANT (OR STRIKE) PRICE.** This is the fixed price of each stock option according to your agreement. Employers

establish it in slightly different ways, but it is usually some derivation of the company's current price, whether the company is public or private.

* **NUMBER OF OPTIONS.** This is the number of stock options included in your agreement, say 100 or 1,000. The amount varies, usually depending on your position.

* **VESTING.** Vesting is the amount of time until the stock options you've been given are available for you to do something with. Usually employers make a portion of the options, say 25 percent each year, available to you. It's like someone saying, "I'm giving you a trip to the four corners of the United Sates, but you only get to see one area of the country per year, so it's going to take four years to go on the whole trip." You might ask, "What's your vesting schedule?" This is simply the timeline under which the stock options are doled out to you, e.g., 25 percent per year for four years.

* **EXERCISING.** This means buying or selling your options once any portion of them is vested. This is when you're reminded that a stock option agreement is an *agreement,* not the real-deal stock certificates. When you exercise, the options are turned into real stock that you can immediately sell (at current market value) or buy (at your grant price) and keep for later.

* **NONQUALIFIED STOCK OPTION.** This is the most common form of employee stock options. Their distinguishing feature is how taxes are dealt with. When you exercise or sell your options you are immediately taxed at your income tax rate.

A Stock Option Story

The best way to explain how stock options work is to give an example. Let's say you decide to take the dream job and get 1,000 stock options at ten dollars a share with a 25-percent-a-year vesting schedule that starts on January 15, 2002. You can't take action on any of your options for at least a year, so you put the agreement in safe keeping. On January 15, 2003, 250 of your stock options are vested, or 25 percent. Currently the stock is selling at eight dollars a share, two dollars below the price of your agreement, so you decide to wait and see whether the market price gets better. In the meantime, you love your job and the people you work with and are establishing a great reputation. Another year goes by and on January 15, 2004, another 250 of your stock options are vested, so now you have 500 vested options total. The market price is now at thirteen dollars a share, which makes you consider exercising your 500 options. Instead you decide to hold on and see whether the price goes higher. Before you know it, January 15, 2005, comes around and another 250 options vest. Now you have a total of 750 vested options, and the public stock price has continued to increase to twenty dollars a share. That's twice your grant price! You're tempted to exercise all your options now to help with the downpayment of your new home, but again you decide to wait because you're involved at more senior levels and you can clearly see that this company is going places. At last, it's January 15, 2006, and you're fully vested. All 1,000 stock options are yours. It's icing on the cake of your new promotion. Three months later you decide it's time to make your move because the stock price has skyrocketed to sixty-five dollars a share. You exercise all of your stock options in a same-day sale transaction: You buy all 1,000 of them at ten dollars a share from the company and immediately turn around and sell them in the public stock market at sixty-five dollars a share. Your profit is fifty-five dollars per share, or $55,000 (less taxes). Talk about a bonus!

Watch Out!

Keep in mind that this story could have gone very differently. The company could have done poorly over time, and their stock could have plummeted to five dollars a share or even less. When weighing the risk of taking stock options in lieu of a higher salary or bonus, remember that stock options are worth taking the risk when you believe the company's stock price will go up, not down. Stock options aren't worth the paper the agreement is written on if the grant price you're given is above the current market price. In this case, they're referred to as being "underwater."

Always check with your tax attorney or accountant before making any decisions about managing your stock options.

----

6. So You've Got the Job. Now What?

Getting the job you want is the first step to the next evolution of your career, perhaps the Now Economy You 2.0. Don't wait for your new boss and colleagues to make you feel comfortable or give direction. That's what often happens and, as a result, we usually feel that things are off to a slow start. Instead, reach out to them first, give them the impression of yourself you want them to have, and start contributing right away. You'll already be on your way to creating the relationships and political support you need to succeed at your new company.

The First Day

* **GO TO THE COMPANY'S ORIENTATION.** Listen to the way the company portrays itself in the materials presented and the people who present them. What are the underlying cultural messages and values? Are they consistent with what you know of the company so far? What behaviors does the company expect of

employees? Does the company have a process for letting employees know what their manager expects from them, such as a performance management or appraisal system? The sooner you understand what's really valued, the sooner you'll know how things operate and how you can use this informal system for yourself. By all means, ask as many questions as you need to be clear on anything covered.

* **MEET WITH YOUR NEW BOSS.** A great boss will have already initiated a meeting with you. However, if he or she has not set up a meeting, take the initiative and ask for at least a brief meeting sometime later that day. Your purpose is to confirm that you're glad to be there, to communicate that you plan to add real value to the team, and to express your desire to be clear on your objectives for the first six months.

* **INTRODUCE YOURSELF TO EVERYONE IN YOUR OFFICE AND IN YOUR DEPARTMENT, FROM RECEPTIONISTS TO ADMINISTRATIVE ASSISTANTS TO TECHNICIANS TO MANAGERS TO SENIOR MANAGERS.** This is your opportunity to create the first impression you want. It's not hard to make the first move. Simply state your name, your role, and that you wanted to say hello. Then ask about their roles (even if you think you know). Undoubtedly, you will get a smile in return because you've communicated respect by this simple, friendly gesture. You are building relationships that may be key to your success there.

The First Week

* **DETERMINE WITH YOUR BOSS SPECIFIC GOALS FOR THE NEXT THREE TO SIX MONTHS.** You want a clear understanding so there's no confusion about your performance or worth. Ask what the perfect result or outcome looks like. Be clear on any resources or restrictions. Make

sure you have some near-term, easy wins so you can quickly show your abilities and contributions.

✳ **HAVE LUNCH WITH AT LEAST THREE DIFFERENT PEOPLE IN YOUR GROUP.** The first-day introduction was a good start; now build on it with a more significant interaction. Make it easy going by asking lots of questions that get them to talk about themselves.

✳ **GET ALL YOUR LOGISTICS SET UP.** Get your phone number, voice mail, computer, network logins, e-mail account, postal mailbox, name badge, parking permit, office supplies, and business cards. Then give your phone number and e-mail address to your group and significant others outside your office.

The First Six Months

✳ **PERFORM.** Deliver on agreed-upon results. Generate at least one or two innovative ideas tied to significant department goals. Gain as much new business knowledge as you can. Competence still counts.

✳ **GET FEEDBACK FROM YOUR BOSS.** How satisfied is he or she with your results? How can you improve? Listen carefully to comments on what you've produced and how.

✳ **TRY TO GET IN FRONT OF YOUR BOSS'S BOSS.** It's much easier to give a fresh impression as the new hire than to be someone unknown who's been around a while. Come up with an idea or information to share that ties to an objective this person is trying to achieve, then ask for a chance to discuss it. Don't be shy about showing up your direct boss; simply make him or her look good in the process.

✳ **BUILD YOUR NETWORK.** Expand beyond your department. Reach out to those you meet in meetings or on project teams who are unfamiliar. Understand who's who and what role they play.

* **ASSESS THE POWER STRUCTURE.** What is political power based on? Knowledge? Creativity? Position? Results? Personal presence? Figure out who's got it, how people get it, and how to use it to help you.

The First Year

* **CONTINUE TO PERFORM.** In the Now Economy, your ability to consistently produce results keeps you in the driver's seat.

* **TRY TO BE A PART OF AT LEAST ONE KEY PROJECT THAT GETS YOU NOTICED AND SHOWS YOUR WORTH TO AN EVER-WIDENING AUDIENCE.** Be able to articulate how the project ties to the company's larger objectives or strategy and your contribution. Openly commend others on the project who achieved results with you.

* **PROPOSE A PERSONAL DEVELOPMENT PROGRAM, SUCH AS TRAINING OR CONFERENCES.** Continuous learning is key in the Now Economy. If you can't get approval in your first year, it's probably not going to happen easily later.

* **CONTINUE TO BUILD YOUR EXTERNAL NETWORK.** Change is the norm of the Now Economy, so you need to be able to shift as circumstances change. Initiate chats with people outside your company, simply to get to know them. You never know who may be your next employer or client. Keep your options open.

One Thing I Wish I'd Understood Before I Quit AOL

6

I TRY not to dwell on this too much. But had I known this sooner, this little bit of intelligence would have been worth at least $100,000 to me, maybe even much more: Office politics is a good thing.

Surprised? So was I as I started wising up. If I had been a little more savvy as to how I could make office politics work for me, I might have stayed at AOL a little longer (if I wanted to, of course). I might have achieved the title of director, or even vice president, before leaving. I would have understood better what my boss meant when he said, "Mary, you're just not strategic enough," and decided to pass me over for a promotion and give the job I was more than qualified for to an outsider. In fact, he never would have had to say that because I would have scoped out well in advance what behaviors my boss particularly valued (especially subconsciously) and performed those behaviors to my (and AOL's, of course) advantage, in addition to my stated job requirements. *That* would have been strategic!

But no; for ten years, I operated as though my job was to get the work done, with passion, and to be a team player in helping AOL realize its big vision: "To build an interactive medium that improves the lives of people and benefits society as no other medium before it."

That's a pretty tall order, if you ask me. Wasn't it enough that I was helping the company change the world, without focusing on distracting, petty little power plays? I mean, really, there are only so many hours in the day! Well, the fact of the matter was, those power plays were happening all around me, whether I liked it or not. And by not bodaciously engaging in them to my benefit, I was disengaged from them to my detriment.

But in my noble naiveté, like any good foot soldier who's not completely concentrating on where she's going, I tripped and fell on my own sword. Was I skewered by someone else's skullduggery? Was this something to blame someone else for? I don't think so. I was just so focused on the greater mission of the work at hand that I didn't take steps to show my boss that I was also capable of strategizing a plan for the future. I wasn't clued into the fact that this is what it would take to impress him. You don't need a nasty conniver to be on the losing side of a political game. You just have to be dedicated completely to your work.

I needed to help my boss regard me in a far more powerful and empowered light. That would have taken some political strategy, and that's the thing I resisted. Office politics seemed so unworthy, so suspicious, so underhanded. Isn't it enough just to help make AOL the leading Internet service provider on the planet? Guess not! I needed to get smart about office politics. And I didn't until it was too late.

Office Politics Isn't Always Pretty, but Snow White and Sleeping Beauty Are

How much would you trust a woman who brags, "I just love office politics!" Not very much, I'd bet. Even I would be very careful about what I said to her in the future. But office politics can be a powerful, positive tool for bodacious women.

Sometimes office politics is not pretty. It goes completely against our good girl coding of being kind, accommodating, self-sacrificing, and forthright. The only behavioral sleight of hand our culture allows women—and that is given to us begrudgingly—is just a touch of romantic trickery. (Personally, I think romance is where you should be especially straightforward.) In fact, a woman who is seen as especially good at office politics is more often vilified. She's categorized as scheming, conniving, untrustworthy, self-centered, opportunistic, disloyal—all the words that especially go against the good girl grain. For hundreds of years, describing someone as an ambitious woman was not at all flattering.

How awful it would be for our coworkers to mistrust us and our core motives! Wouldn't it be better for us to be virtuous, simple, trusted, and just plain good at what we do, regardless of the sacrifice of our potential growth and success that we must suffer? And worse, how awful it would be if we actually tried to pull a fast one and failed! It would be the cosmic comeuppance we would feel that we deserved. We'd have to endure whispers behind our back: "She got what she deserved." It's so much better to play it safe, play it good, and, as a result, play it with self-imposed limitations.

It's not surprising that most of us don't know how to do politics. As little girls, especially in the United States, we had no positive female role models in office politics. No one does. For guys, it's not flattering to be called a "yes man." But women especially don't have support in developing their political acumen. Think of our earliest models of women: Sleeping Beauty and Snow White. They were celebrated for their gentle, innocent presence. In fact, at least according to the Disney version, so innocent, so trustworthy, so harmless were they that they moved through life completely oblivious to anything wicked happening around them. Their very goodness (partly manifested by their physical beauty) was their meal ticket. And the creatures of the forest scampered trustingly up to them and sat admiringly at their feet while they whistled and danced and gazed into wells and waited for something to happen to them. Something happened to them, all right. They both got snookered by seriously ambitious wicked witches.

(I'd like to point out here that most of the creatures of the Disney forest were gentle vegetarians: the bunnies, the deer, the squirrels, the birdies, all of whom are at the bottom of the forest's organizational food chain. Now imagine Sleeping Beauty waltzing with a grizzly! How great it would be to command the respect of a creature that could reduce you to fettuccine with one swipe of a paw. Now *that* would be bodacious!)

So here they are hanging out with the Animal Kingdom's support staff and misfits (those seven guys aren't exactly fast-track material), not having their potential tested in an especially challenging way, and counting on their beauty and youthful innocence to get them what they want to lead a fulfilling life. They are not becoming bodacious.

But soon they fall into the evil hands of ambition. Snow White's nemesis is jealous of her beauty and comes up with the apple gambit. Now Snow, in her innocence, bites into the apple and is thus iced (instead of fired) until Prince Charming happens by with preheated lips.

Sleeping Beauty has a slightly more bodacious and political twist. In fact, this might be the young girl's first introduction to a little wink-wink, nod-nod workplace political intrigue. Here we are at the princess's first birthday party, the power reception of the year. Everyone who's anyone is invited. Except for one: the wicked witch. An oversight, to be sure, but the damage is done. Some people are so touchy! Of course, she comes anyway. Eleven fairies step up to the crib and bestow on the baby all the virtues necessary to flesh out any princess's résumé: looks, smarts, wit, cash. The youngest fairy, having procrastinated, has nothing to offer (not a good career move).

So she lets the wicked witch announce her gift next. Well, the witch totally vents, says something pretty threatening about a prick and a demise and then flounces off in a snit.

This is where the youngest fairy gets political. It's actually the best part of the story. She waits until the witch is out of hearing distance (smart thinking), and then to the assembled party (which isn't much of a party anymore—there's nothing like a curse to ruin everything) she says, "Look, I can't do much about the curse. That would be going over her head. But I can reduce the fine just a tad. Instead of the princess being dead for, like, ever, let's make it, say, 100 years. Okay? And just so you don't miss anything, I'll knock everyone out on her twenty-first birthday, and lock up the place with some briars. After a century has gone by, a prince will come along and break the spell, and everyone will rise and shine. The yardman might have some cleaning up to do, but that will be it. In the meantime, keep Her Highness away from sharp things. How's that?"

This is a very bodacious and political fairy. She waits until the coast is clear to make her move. She doesn't pause to ask permission. She leverages her talents to their utmost capacity, she dares to change the course of events launched by someone further up the organizational chart, and she courageously speaks up before the entire community. She puts her little fairy foot down and says, "No! The future will not go that way, it will go this way!"

Talk about garnering some major points with the king!

The youngest fairy is the best part of the story. But we tend to dismiss her contributions as just a nice thing to have done, one of those nurturing, caretaking services all women are expected to perform. We overlook her while marveling at the wicked witch's evil connivings, the princess's beauty, and the prince's dashing heroics. What she did was political, pure and simple. And she saved the day! But if this fairy came up to you in your cube and confided, "I just love office politics, don't you?" you'd probably make a mental note to not invite her to any of your parties. I know I would. But think what would have happened without her!

Politics Is Our Friend

Politics is like bats. Both are mysterious and unpredictable. They operate under cover of darkness and seem to come out of nowhere. And we worry that they'll make a nest in our hair. They get terrible press. But given half the chance, bats perform a valuable service: They eat mosquitoes, those terrible bloodsuckers that do nothing for humanity but cause misery. Politics can do the same kind of service for a company and a career. Properly used, politics strengthens the company, improves the workplace environment, and neutralizes the parasites (ineffective, unhelpful people, programs, and policies) that threaten to compromise the vitality and rewards of pursuing the corporate mission. We somehow became culturally coded to shudder at the thought of the very thing that could make the difference between a career (or company) that fails and one that doesn't.

Imagine your first day in a new position. You're sitting at your desk, arranging the pictures and pencil holder. You're just about to adjust your monitor position when you notice someone at the door. You recognize him as one of the members of the department you just joined. He looks both ways down the corridor and then steps into your office like he's ducking spiderwebs. "Listen," he says as he reaches for a chair, "I just thought I'd warn you, this place is really political. I figured you might as well know now. Okay? Well, bye. Oh! and welcome!"

And you're left sitting behind your desk, your mouth open to ask a question you hadn't really formulated in your mind yet, but now there's no one to ask. He's gone. How do you feel? My guess is that you'd be thinking, "Oh my God, I've fallen into a nest of vipers. The rules won't be clear. There's probably already someone out to get me. The boss plays favorites, and there will be subtext and backstory with everything. And since I'm so new I won't be clued in. I'm already doomed to fail, and I haven't even started yet!"

Well, here's some news: Every workplace is political, and the higher up the organizational chart you go, the more political the workplace gets. That's because there's more at stake. The higher up you go, the more things get accomplished by virtue of relationships and positioning. Think about it. Entry-level, frontline positions, such as customer service reps and junior programmers, typically don't get caught up in high-level, complex positioning and angling for power. Serving the customer is job-one-and-only. In a very important way, the company vision is never so clear and pure as at that level. It's usually as you rise through the ranks that ego, hidden agenda, and compromise show up. As there's more to gain, there's also more to lose. And everyone is doing what's necessary to make sure that doesn't happen to them.

So the good news is this: The more you start feeling besieged by politics, the higher up the ranks you're climbing. Doesn't that make you feel better?

Well, here's some more news: "Office politics" is just another way to spell "leadership." And that's a good thing! Like leadership, political acumen is the technique and art of making people feel good about themselves while they are helping you. It is a form of plugged-in power that is created when we are trusted and have built a track record that says, "You can count on me." We may use the strategies of office politics to gain a competitive advantage in our own careers. But in most cases we gain from office politics only if what we do ultimately benefits the company, its employees, and its stakeholders in the long run.

On a day-to-day basis, office politics can:

* Allow people at all levels of the organization to move up and around, because politics can give them the opportunity to get recognized.

* Help managers support their employees by acquiring the resources they need to get the job done and serve as a buffer between the employees and distracting pressures from higher-ups.

* Help the company as a whole succeed as senior-level leaders use politics to cultivate support and enthusiasm for company initiatives, both internally and in the outside community.

But like anything misused or overused, politics has a downside. In an unhealthy political environment that breeds distrust, politics can:

* Focus employees inward to protect their own turf rather than outward on the customer. The customer suffers, and the company's health is diminished by employees who are so busy looking over their shoulders that they're not paying attention to the work at hand.

* Put too much focus on form and image and take the emphasis away from substance and content. Without substance— and without any assurance that substance is on its way—investors and employees rapidly lose faith in the company. This is even more the case in the Now Economy, as investors have learned some hard lessons in recent years from dot.com stock.

* Deprive just reward to people who are so focused on contributing to an organization's success and development that they neglect their personal clout and competitive position inside the company. It happens all the time. Without at least one antenna tuned to the political scene, you can be so focused on the job that you can sabotage your career.

That's an easy mistake to make, especially in a company where the mission is so all-absorbing and demanding. And in AOL's early days, I made that mistake. The trouble was that to some extent I continued to make it.

How to Tell Whether Someone's Playing Power Games With You

The Bodacious Woman knows that the more power she has, the more other people are going to want that power. Her bodacious friends will simply ask her for her secrets and advice, but unbodacious people will try to steal it from her. The workplace is full of petty people who don't understand that in the Now Economy political power lies in what you share, not what you grab.

So the Bodacious Woman needs to be alert to these subtle (or not so subtle) power games:

* Your opponent initiates meetings with you but insists that you come to his or her office. If the person is your boss or ranks higher in the organization, this is appropriate. But if the person is your equal or below you in the organization, he or she should come to you or you should meet in some neutral territory such as a conference room or cafeteria.

* Your opponent often keeps you waiting.

* Your opponent repeatedly rejects your ideas and insists on new ones in a rapid-fire, high-pressure atmosphere.

* Your opponent is always looking down on you. Some people maneuver themselves and their office furniture to make sure they are always at least at eye level or higher than you are. They're angling for height advantage because they feel at a disadvantage in other, more important ways.

* Your opponent touches you too frequently or inappropriately. Your opponent doesn't have to touch you in any sensitive body areas to be out of line.

> Too frequent is too familiar, which sends a mes-
> sage of a one-up–one-down relationship.
>
> * Your opponent has a blank expression. To show no
> expression at all during a conversation is just plain
> bizarre. If you see a poker face on the person you're
> trying to have a conversation with, you can safely
> assume he or she is struggling to keep important
> thoughts hidden.
>
> How do you respond to these power plays? That's up
> to your personal style and relationship with your oppo-
> nent. What's important is that you identify other people's
> strategies to manipulate your feelings of confidence and
> self-worth. It's also important that as you discover situa-
> tional feelings of insecurity or inadequacy, you remember
> to take a mental step back and see that it's probably some
> power play your opponent is trying to work on you. This
> is your bodacious advantage.

(Office) Size Still Matters

From the day I showed up at Quantum in my little blue seersucker suit, I leveraged my good girl ethic. Work hard. Be trustworthy. Be fair. Produce. People will notice. And in the early days, they did. That was when the company was simple, at least at the level I was working in. There were so few of us, the ones who produced got noticed and rewarded. Everyone was focused on the same mission: to make AOL a marvelous service and to thrive, despite what the market, the experts, and the headlines were predicting. Do an out-standing job and you had your ticket to advancement. Being a good girl worked for me.

It stopped working around 1997, but I was too good a girl to notice. When I finally did, it was too late. One of the biggest and hardest lessons for me was realizing that although those below me in the organization still supported the "perform well and you'll get promoted" rule of behavior, the ones immediately above me were operating according to a different set of rules: "I assume you're going to perform well unless you prove otherwise. What I want to know now is what else you can offer." My big mistake was that I didn't put the time, energy, and creativity into answering that "what else" question and then promoting myself for all I was worth.

The change in political environment wasn't just about my own upward trek through the power layers. There was an important shift within AOL as well, a shift that affects every start-up as it matures, grows, and finally begins to act like an established company. It was growing up just as I was growing up. I was practically homegrown from within AOL's incubator, along with many of the ragtag mavericks who launched this vision. But around 1995 AOL was hiring thousands and thousands of new employees, many of whom came to the company not only professionally competent but also politically savvy. I may have had the years of organizational knowledge, but I knew nothing about the buy-and-sell world of power brokering. Compared with the outside experiences these new employees brought to AOL, I had no real sense of the subtext of intrigue and positioning they were also bringing into the company.

And for most of those years, that was just fine. My value to the company was in the relationship, organizational knowledge, and personal skills I brought to the workplace. I was too busy to realize that political savvy was becoming an increasingly important power to have.

Just how far out of touch I was with this important fact of life occurred to me in 1997 when the AOL campus near the Dulles International Airport was being developed. Offices and cubicles were assigned not by efficiency or the amount of space each employee needed but by title. I thought, "How ridiculous!"

What a contrast to just a few years earlier when my manager, the call center director, preferred to have his workspace in the middle of the floor so he was in the flow of activity and modeling the "we're all in this together" attitude that he wanted from his employees. I knew when his boss finally insisted that he have the largest corner office with windows that we were entering a new phase where a different kind of symbolism was needed. As humans we tend to want a leader to look up to (and criticize when things don't go well). And having prime physical space represented that importance. Still, a part of me was saddened by the loss of leadership purity that this new value represented.

Of course, I had my own saga of office spaces and how they represented my changing status within AOL. Over the slightly more than ten years I was with AOL, I had more than ten workspaces, ranging from open cubicles that I shared with other people who covered different shifts to semiprivate cubicles to all sizes of offices. As I moved through them, I saw the advantage of each situation, but I never allowed myself to connect the space with stature—just the workload and the environment I needed to get it done. I appreciated the privacy of offices when I was creating and writing training materials. I enjoyed the openness and sociability of the cubicles. By the time I landed my own office with a pond view, I began to appreciate what it meant to have such a space. And I really knew what value it held when I lost it.

In losing my bid for the promotion to director, I also lost the wonderful office, which was reassigned to the man who was hired from the outside to fill that role. I knew that once I lost that office and was relegated to the cubicle outside it, I would lose some political status. Newcomers immediately associated my workspace with a much lower organizational level, giving me a limitation I wasn't used to.

Losing the office symbolized a greater loss. I lost the battle to realize my dreams to continue to rise through the ranks of a company I cared deeply about. But in a larger sense I won something more valuable: I won the chance to explore a new bodacious self in a larger world.

Strategies From the Political Masters

No one likes to admit that they enjoy office politics, but there is one group of experts who don't mind political intrigue at all and don't mind you knowing it, either: professional politicians. Presidents,

representatives, senators, and their various aides and the other professionals who play this particular game make no bones about what
they do. In fact, they're *expected* to engage in the finer techniques of
getting things accomplished through relationships. And their examples are out there for all of us to learn from.

STRATEGY 1: KNOW WHAT WINNING MEANS TO YOU

Bodacious women ask, "How do you win?" (We're presuming that
winning involves playing by at least the important moral rules.)
After all, that's what you want to do, right? But what exactly does
winning look like to you? Do you know why you're competing in
the first place? Is this particular game worth your time and attention? Or is there a different game going on somewhere else with
better prizes?

Remember the first time you sat down to a board game with
your family and you first started hearing talk about winning?
"What do I get if I win?" you might have asked. "Nothing," your
family probably said. "Just the satisfaction of doing your best."
That might have been enough over a friendly game of Candyland.
But in the grown-up world, although doing your best certainly
holds personal satisfaction, your concept of winning must be far
more compelling and unambiguous for you. Unless you know what
you're playing for and what your win looks like, you won't even
know whether you really won it.

You have a choice of macro-wins and micro-wins, depending on
the political challenge that's in front of you. The micro-wins are
the short-term prizes that you can see every day or are extended
out a few months into the future at the most. A micro-win can
position you for a plum project, cultivate a friendship that will
open powerful doors, give you the opportunity to present to a
group senior to your boss, net you an assistant, furnish your office
with new, upscale furniture, get you an invitation to an important
reception where you can buttonhole an important player in your
larger strategy, or get your tuition fully reimbursed. A micro-win
is being able to achieve all these things gracefully and ethically,

gathering valuable support above and below you, without being called the short B-word. (Some envious others might call you the short B-word anyway, but you know better.)

And if you're energy efficient, micro-wins accumulate to help you achieve the macro-wins. The macro-wins may include your long-term goals to climb through the ranks of a single company and eventually achieve a senior executive position. Or you might gain more and more influence in a personally meaningful cause so that you become its prominent spokesperson. Or maybe your long-term win might be becoming a widely recognized industry expert, giving you a broader field of opportunities, an opportunity for a kind of celebrity (every specialization has its stars), with an expertise-based passport that opens a wide variety of doors for you. Maybe your idea of a macro-win is a combination of all. In fact, the bodacious strategy would be to use each to leverage your ability to boost the other. At any rate, these are long-term, large-scale macro-wins, where the results of your invested efforts and relationship building may not be immediately apparent.

Investing some of your daily focus on the macro-wins is an important part of your political strategy that will help you make key balancing decisions as to whether one particularly tempting short-term gain (the micro-win) is worth the possible damage to the macro-win you have your eye on. This is the mistake that causes so many women to be labeled "bitches" and so many men to be called "yes men." Immediate gratification can cost big in terms of long-term benefits. On the other hand, some macro-wins can be put off in favor of a booster shot of much-needed micro-wins. For example, at the last minute you hear about an important conference that is bringing together some industry powerhouses. That could be a macro-win for you, but it conflicts with a previously scheduled family vacation. You may be tempted to postpone the vacation in favor of the conference. But these conferences happen all the time; you can go to the next one. Keeping promises that you make to your family is a one-shot deal. Miss that shot and it's a major loss on both macro and micro levels.

Know what you want before going after it politically. And know how going after it could affect your other envisioned wins, both macro and micro.

STRATEGY 2: UNDERSTAND YOUR POWER BASE

The core of office politics is power and how you use it through leadership to get things done. How effective you are in office politics reflects how you leverage the various points of power that are always available to you (in different proportions, of course, depending on where you are organizationally as well as in your career and in popularity).

Knowledge Power: What You Know

In the Now Economy, knowledge power can bring you the big bucks early in your career, especially in the high-tech arena. AOL and other Internet and high-tech companies pay a premium for qualified technical employees and then treat them like demigods, doing whatever it takes to keep them from jumping ship. New entrants starting out in the high-tech fields make several times the salary their parents had when they retired. If you're largely motivated by money and have an aptitude for technology, knowledge power is excellent political capital for you to use to invest in your future.

But you don't have to be a techie to capitalize on your own knowledge power, although it may take a little longer to use it to its full capacity. Other kinds of knowledge power will give you political leverage on the job:

* *Organizational knowledge.* This was power I could have leveraged more. After ten years at AOL I was like Radar O'Reilly on *M*A*S*H*. I knew how to get just about anything anyone needed. I knew just about everyone who was anyone. I knew both the written and the unwritten rules about how things were done. It's because of my organizational knowledge that I was asked to find a way to get a high response rate to the company's first employee opinion

survey. I remember my boss saying, "Mary, you know how this place works better than anyone else. Make it happen." And I did. Again and again.

* *Content knowledge.* If you are able to find a passion early and steep yourself in it as a child, by the time you're ready to market that passion commercially, you've outpaced your competition before even starting. Think about filmmakers such as Steven Spielberg and Ron Howard. By the time they were young men, they were ready to hit the ground running. But if you're like most people I know, it's taken you time and some meandering down different paths to find your passion. Once you find it, you can't help wanting to learn everything you can. And you don't have to throw out what you've learned to date. You can often apply parts of it to the expertise you're gaining.

* *Industry knowledge.* Maybe you're not as intrigued by the content, but you know how a particular industry works. You know the ropes, how business is transacted, who the key players are, how to favorably position a company or product or service, what the industry trends are, and how to close deals. You love the process, bringing all the elements together to make things happen. That's powerful! Your knowledge is golden because it's the way business often gets done.

* *Behavioral knowledge.* There's knowledge power in knowing how people prefer to be treated. If your previous boss liked to have weekly progress reports but your current boss despises them, how happy do you think you'd be if you continued behaving in the old way? For that matter, how long do you think you would be employed? Or maybe you know that your project partner is under an unusual amount of personal stress, and you can discreetly pick up some of her extra work while she copes with the problem. That's powerful

insight that you can use one day to meet one of your macro-level visions. By being sensitive to the private needs of your team now, you will build a form of group loyalty that you can bring with you as you launch that bodacious start-up of your own.

Creative Power: How You Apply What You Know

Knowledge is like a great computer or kitchen appliance. It may look pretty and impressive, but it won't do a darn bit of good until you plug it into an outlet. The ways you apply what you know—all those different outlets—range from what companies you choose to work for, what projects you are able to participate in, and what start-ups you choose to create. This is no longer an information economy; it's an imagination economy. How we move forward depends completely on how creatively we reassemble the bits and pieces of ideas, facts, contacts, and what we read in the newspaper this morning to come up with new, effective ideas that no one has ever seen before.

We may already be on information overload. And maybe we do multiply the amount of data we have exponentially every several years or so. But roomfuls of data are completely meaningless if you don't have fresh, interesting, and profitable ways to organize those data and bring them to market. Cultivate a reputation as a smart idea person, and almost anyone will take your call. People will always want to know what's on your mind.

Positional Power: What Your Rank Is

Your job title will open doors. The company you work for is also an association that will open doors. But you have to be willing to use that position as leverage to make those things happen for you. It doesn't matter how high up you are or are not in your company, there will be people who look to you precisely for the role you play in the company, your access to certain people, and your unique ability to make things happen in your particular corner of the business. Remember, if your position wasn't a vital part of the overall business plan, it would not have been created. If you hadn't been the best candidate for that position, you never would have been hired for it. If you have risen through the ranks within the same company, you have more than earned your position. It belongs to you. You've proven yourself again and again. So claim the political power that comes with it. And use it!

Relationship Power: Who You Know

"It isn't what you know, it's who you know." That saying usually is delivered with resentment, sarcasm, and cynicism. What is so wrong with leveraging your contacts, the power that comes with them, and the respect they hold for you? As we explored in Chapter Three, this is one of the joys of being in business in the Now Economy! More than ever before, we can bring our true selves to the workplace and reach our associates' hearts with our authenticity. The workplace is the new community, and people are excited by the spark of individuality we contribute to projects we care about.

One of the best things about relationship power is that often we don't use it on our own behalf. We use it for the benefit of others. Matching talents and passions by building relationships simply won't work if we don't bring our own authentic contributions to the table and offer them generously for the good of the group.

The next time someone asks you to facilitate an introduction, do it (unless, of course, that person is an embarrassment to you). What you know is meaningless unless you can use it to help other people and make projects happen.

Personal Power: Your Relationship With Yourself

It's not the successful presentation before the venture capitalist that makes or breaks dreams. Nor is it the it-was-meant-to-happen job interview. The first hurdle for success happens between your ears. Does your self-talk dismantle every good idea you have and discourage you from taking it public? If it does, there is some comfort in knowing that you're not alone. But there's no future in it either.

As we've talked about before, our self-esteem is one of the biggest barriers to entry for us as we try to achieve careers that capitalize on our entire potential, pay us what we're worth, and broaden our horizons. Do any of these lines ring a familiar bell?

"I don't feel right pointing out my accomplishments. That sounds like bragging to me."

"Maybe I'd get more respect if I looked better."

"What did I say that would cause him to turn on me like that?"

"In some ways it would have been better if I had lost the job instead of her. She needs the work more than I do."

"I get embarrassed so easily. Not only by my own actions but by others' as well."

"I know I shouldn't go for that new opportunity. I haven't worked hard enough."

"Well, if my ideas were any good, someone would have already thought of it and spoken up by now. I'd better keep mum."

Alan Weiss, author of the book *Million Dollar Consulting*, says this: "Your first sale must be to yourself." If you're not a happy customer, don't blame yourself for that too. You've just had more than your fair share of negative self-talk tapes installed in your soul. Be proud to seek out the counseling you need to step onto the bodacious world stage. There's no shame, and looking for help isn't a sign of weakness. You're just taking another step toward the authentic self you not only deserve to be but need to be. The Now Economy won't settle for anything less.

STRATEGY 3: KNOW YOUR PLATFORM

Politicians know what they stand for—at least what they stand for now. You can always change when it's strategically wise to do so, as long as it's authentic. Famous politicians have been known to change parties. Ronald Reagan, believe it or not, was once a Democrat.

The old expression goes like this: "Know what you stand for or you'll fall for anything." Knowing what you stand for, and then letting others know it too, is an important aspect of branding. What do you stand for in your career? Meaningful work that will benefit millions? The drive to work for a company that is likely to go public and make you a millionaire? The mission of helping the company you work for develop family-friendly human resource policies? Working for a company that is environmentally friendly or that has progressive international corporate citizenship principles? All of the above?

What is your "domestic" policy? What do you stand for within the workplace? Can people count on you to keep a secret? To respect deadlines? To go to bat for them when their own issues are at stake? Are you known for being fair and open? Are you known for the skill with which you curry favor from more senior and powerful people? Are you a great communicator? Or do you emerge from your closed office in the late afternoon looking vaguely guilty? When people wonder what you've been up to, can they count on it being good, whatever it might be?

When you know what your platform is, market it! Obviously you can't stand at the back end of a train car speaking into a microphone before a cheering crowd. But there are excellent and effective ways to push forward your message and position yourself in just the right spotlight:

* Use your e-mail signature line to publish a favorite quote that summarizes your perspective or brand.

* When distributing progress reports, tie your accomplishments to your platform whenever possible.

* Lend meaningful books to friends on the subjects that are most important to you. For instance, I would never have latched on to the concept of being bodacious if not for Tiane Mitchell-Gordon at AOL, who demonstrated through her words and actions that I could trust her with the most troubling secrets of my personal life and shared with me two of her favorite books by SARK, who celebrates the bodacious life.

* If you don't like gossip, don't engage in it yourself. Eventually people will notice that you don't spread it around. But they just might give you all those valuable insights and trade secrets they're dying to tell someone!

* Be seen at important events, private and public, that support initiatives and causes that are important to you. Volunteer your services for special interest groups that support the principles you hold most important.

Behave consistently with your message and you will soon be known for your platform.

STRATEGY 4: LEARN THE ART OF LOBBYING

How do you suppose all those elected officials come to understand the intricate details of controversies, issues, and national policies? Hired experts prowl the halls of the legislative offices throughout the country (not just Washington, DC) and grab these policy makers every chance they get to pass on another insight or message. This is why they're called lobbyists: They used to hang out in the lobbies of congressional office buildings.

Today lobbying is done in much the same way, although modern lobbyists are paid far too much to stand around in lobbies waiting for a representative on her way to a vote. It's done in a much more sophisticated manner these days: receptions, letter-writing campaigns, model bills, and drawing on the currency of long-standing friendships. Other people (volunteers who are equally—if not more—passionate about the issue) do the hall crawling, visiting offices, sitting down with a legislative aide (or the representative, if the volunteer is lucky or important enough), and articulating the message for the umpteenth time.

The famous "elevator speech" is an example of Now Economy corporate lobbying. You can grab the attention of key players by having a really good three-minute presentation prepared, being ready to take advantage of the happenstance meeting in the ladies' room or fitness center. You can even find out what that person's favorite civic organizations are and take advantage of the coincidental meeting ("Fancy meeting you here!"). This may sound unseemly and scheming, but it's not if the cause is so important to you that you're willing to do just about anything to help it go forward. Just be sure you can sleep at night and look at yourself in the mirror the next day.

STRATEGY 5: LEARN THE ART OF COMPROMISE

You may not be able to get all that you want. Know how much less you'd be willing to settle for. Know the difference between your nonnegotiables and negotiables. Know where you would draw the line between *deal* and bad deal. Would you be willing to forgo the promotion this time if you knew you'd be first on the list the next time, and if you took part in certain key projects in the meantime? Do you have the nerve to ask for that deal in writing? (Your boss may not be your boss anymore by the time next time rolls around, so only you would be there to remember the deal.)

You may not get everything you want in a certain arrangement, but you will get some of what you want if you learn to compromise. Learn to compromise well, and the part you do get will be the part you want the most.

STRATEGY 6: LEARN GRACEFUL DEFEAT

Some of the time you won't get even part of what you want. You will lose completely. It will be humiliating. It may even feel devastating. You might even feel betrayed by your boss, who said he'd support you and then didn't. You'll feel as though you don't belong in the company anymore. Maybe you'll even start considering grad school!

No defeat is truly an utter, complete defeat. How you carry yourself through the agonizing "chin up" time could speak volumes about you to the powerful people who are watching. The opportunities that might result from a new level of respect and admiration could be better than anything you imagined.

Graceful defeat is helping the person who got the job instead of you become successful in his new job. Graceful defeat is pleasantly surprising your boss, who is expecting you to be in a huge snit over the disappointment. Graceful defeat is saying through your actions, "I can't do much about the curse, but I can reduce the fine just a tad. No one will blame me for behaving poorly. But that's not going to happen. I'm going to act with dignity and self-respect."

But don't get too graceful with your defeats. If they start getting too comfortable and familiar because you've had a lot of them, you're being defeated way too often. And it's time to rethink your strategy.

The Art of Quitting Well

The Now Economy can feel like a bunch of ups and downs on a dirt road full of potholes and rocks. It's so easy to get caught up in how it feels that we forget that life—plants, animals, the solar system—is a constant experience of cycles. It's just that today's environment has sped up each cycle. (Chaos Theory, which captures the feeling of constant change, is now being called Complexity Theory. Sometimes changing our terminology is one of the first steps to changing how we think about it.)

With constant change there's always a cycle of beginning and ending. We love beginnings and the entrepreneurial spirit that comes with them. We often hate endings and shy away from them, dealing with them only when and to the extent that we have to. Even if you hate your job and can't wait to get away, there's almost always a feeling of loss from the separation. You just want it over with. But you benefit yourself and others by bringing proper closure to your connection.

A common ending in the Now Economy is quitting your job and moving on to another company, going out on your own, or even retiring. But there is also a returning, with people boomeranging back to previous employers. Learning to do it well is a necessary skill. Quitting well is an art, not a science. Here are some ideas about how to be a brilliant artist:

* **LEAVE ON THE BEST POSSIBLE TERMS TO HELP YOU IN THE FUTURE, OR AT LEAST NOT HARM YOU.** Your involvement with that company is part of your employment history. If you leave on good terms you increase your chances of getting positive references for future employers or clients. Your former employer might be a client one day.

* **DON'T TRY TO RESOLVE ANY NEGATIVE EMOTIONS THROUGH THE QUITTING PROCESS.** You probably won't get any lasting satisfaction from storming into your boss's office and exclaiming, "I'm outta here!" Momentary pleasure, yes. Lasting, no.

* **DEAL WITH ANY ILL FEELINGS THROUGH OUT-OF-OFFICE MEANS.** Talk it out with a friend, take some time away, or write a flame letter and then ball it up and throw it across the room. Remember, your best revenge is leaving and being happier elsewhere.

* **SHOW RESPECT.** Inform your direct manager before anyone else.

* **PLAN FOR INDIVIDUAL PARTINGS.** Ask those who have been most meaningful to you (a supportive colleague or an important power person) to meet one on one—for lunch, for dinner, over coffee, or without food at all. Just by asking, you've communicated how much you appreciate them. They'll probably make time for you.

* **MAKE YOUR LAST WORDS COUNT.** Emphasize the positive when saying goodbye: something you appreciate, some benefit you gained from your association with that company or person, and something positive about your future. Short and sweet works well and is memorable.

> *** TELL PEOPLE HOW TO GET IN TOUCH WITH YOU.** Give your contact information to those you want to stay in touch with, and be the first one to reach out and say hello once you've left.

Voodoo Politics

No chapter on office politics would be complete without a little discussion about the bad stuff, the elusive feeling that you're shadow boxing with the devil and that no matter how hard you swing, you only end up hurting yourself. In fact, the harder you swing, the more you hurt yourself.

Let's face it, in this kind of bad mojo, you're an amateur. As naive as this may sound, it's much better for you to focus on what you do best (providing real value to the company or the project) and let the chips fall where they may for the rest. Those who will appreciate your work will see your work (as long as you market your work). And those are really the only people who count in the new world of bodacious women. Worst case scenario: The evil one manages to scheme and scam all the way to the top of the organization, leaving you and your career in the dust. You know what? If scheming and scamming nets that kind of easy access to the power center, you're better off taking your talents elsewhere anyway. Just be sure to keep your good relationships there intact, in case there is a time you ever return as a customer, client, or contractor.

Which is what I did.

7

Breaking Through to Bodaciousness

BACK IN Chapter Two, "Bodaciousness Starts on the Inside," I showed you how it feels to be bodacious. I used words such as *hope, serenity, confidence,* and *control.* That chapter reflects the inner climate of the bodacious woman. Does it mean that she never panics? Never gets anxious? Never is confused or feels as though she received the short end of the stick now and then? No. But it does mean that it will happen less often, and she has a better way to cope with those feelings. And when she does prevail, her successes pave the way to progress rather than mere survival.

Bodaciousness doesn't happen overnight; it's a process. With each new opportunity to choose the

Bodacious Way, with each new challenge to your courage and your ability and willingness to say "yes" when you want to and "no" when you want to, with each time you put a stake in the ground and take a stand, you are building your bodacious muscle. Whether you work for a company or work for yourself, you are demonstrating that what you do makes a strategic difference. As you better understand and unapologetically articulate how your job relates to the corporate bottom line, you are better able to market yourself in real financial, bodacious, beneficial terms, which is the best offense in a layoff-ridden world. As you continue to apply the principles in this book, you'll see that the changes—even the frightening ones— that unfold in your life can usher you into better circumstances: a better job, a more desirable home, better relationships, a better array of more attractive choices.

Bodaciousness is high-performance living. As bodaciousness improves your internal climate, it also shows up very quickly on the outside. As you become more relaxed, confident, and certain of the outcomes you're trying to achieve through your changed behavior and, most importantly, your perceptions about yourself, those changes manifest themselves in huge strides in your life as a whole. They'll show up in small and large ways. Even better, because you are becoming more strategically oriented and more planning oriented, you will also be equipped to notice those changes and then congratulate yourself. When you clearly define your objectives and focus on them, you will be more prepared to observe when you have achieved those goals, identify what works for you, and build on those successes again and again.

This is a huge improvement over the unbodacious way, which is to focus on what's wrong and not give yourself a moment's peace until all your problems have been solved, which will never happen. In your unbodacious moments, you get caught up in value-based criticisms: Do you deserve to put your work down to enjoy an activity? Do you deserve to be physically fit and look great in clothes? Do you deserve to take that seat at the conference table? Do you deserve to have a happy marriage? And the unbodacious answer is, "Of course not!

How could you?" In the unbodacious world, there's always something to improve, to work on, to create, to serve, to fix before you can really enjoy life and feel proud of who you've become.

But the bodacious answer is, "Bring it on!"

As life strategist Phil McGraw says, "Life is something to be managed, not cured." The Bodacious Way is to manage the various aspects of our lives and by plan to give ourselves the successes, benefits, and pleasures that are in store for us. When this happens, it shows up in your life in changes that are observable not only by you but also by the people around you. Becoming bodacious is a process, and it happens at different rates in different ways with different people in different aspects of their lives. But the overall result of how bodacious women experience life is remarkably similar. Keep at it and here's what you have to look forward to.

The Choices You Make and Actions You Take Will Be Based on Strategy, Not Survival

I have said in this book that the Now Economy is your time to decide who you want to be and then create a strategy to be just that. This is true even when the Now Economy is looking dicey. Actually, this is especially true during iffy times. As Martha and I were completing this manuscript, the Now Economy headlines were not as promising as they were a year ago. The days of what Alan Greenspan called "irrational exuberance" have come to a definite end. But does this doesn't mean we must return to the limited, fear-based ways of grabbing at the first shred of hope that comes floating by in hopes that it will keep us afloat for a little while longer. Just the opposite: Now's the time to get really strategic and plan for the times ahead. And Now Economy business magazines have agreed! Here are some of the cover headlines that appeared in March 2001: "Position Yourself *Now* for Better Times Ahead," "Seven Winning Business Strategies for the Long Haul," "Get Well Now!," "Don't Cut Back—Think Ahead (And Act Fast!)," and "Strategy! (Now More Than Ever)."

As you progress along the Bodacious Way, you'll discover that you are making more choices according to your design for your own future. Tough decisions will be smoothed out because your priorities will speak louder. Your bodacious strategy will help you decide whether and why to pick one assignment over another. Your bodacious strategy will help you determine whose advice to seek out. Your bodacious strategy will govern the time line of your goals and objectives. It's possible that Now Economy events might throw a kink in your plans, and it's possible that you might get laid off or that your company might disappear. And it would be upsetting if that happens. But those events won't knock you off your bodacious path. Why? Because you will have seen it coming and you will already have tactics in place to respond bodaciously to any bad news.

The Now Economy is about change, pure and simple. Respond to that change using your own bodacious strategy and you will thrive. As Harvard Business School professor Michael Porter said in the March 2001 issue of *Fast Company* (p. 154), "Strategy is about making choices, trade-offs; it's about deliberately choosing to be different."

Being bodacious is about being deliberate.

You Are More Aware of What's Happening in You and Around You, and You Use This Information Constructively

Before you can respond to a challenge, yearning, or urge, you are aware that it's happening and what that feeling represents. As you progress up the bodacious path you become more aware of what's happening inside you, and you strategically educate yourself to correctly interpret those feelings. That hankering for the piece of chocolate cake in the fridge: Is it really about hunger or even the desire for the sweet taste? Or is it really about some joy you're feeling and want to celebrate? Or is it about anger? Or excitement? Or frustration? Or maybe you're simply thirsty and you've been misinterpreting your body's message to give it water. Or maybe you're finally noticing that bone-deep fatigue telling you that you need a full night's sleep. Being bodacious, you'll notice the sensation and deliberately decide what it really means so you know how to take care of yourself.

When you're bodacious, you're tuned in to what your body is telling you. You notice the long periods of time when you're concentrating so hard that you're holding your breath. You notice the back pains, the stomach pains, their frequency, and what changes may be happening that you need to see a doctor for. Or maybe your gut reaction is sending out an urgent signal: "Don't take that job!" or "Don't go out with that guy!" or "Make that phone call!" You know to listen to and respect those signals, even if you don't immediately know what's behind them. You trust that eventually you'll understand what that signal was all about and be grateful that you trusted your intuition.

But even as you notice these signals, you will also seek to back them up with relevant data. By being more aware of what your body is saying to you, you are also getting instructions on where to do your research. What areas are relevant to your objectives? Nutrition? Investment? Fitness? Spiritual growth? Market projections related to your particular industry or profession?

You are also more aware of what works for others; you observe the people you admire, take mental notes on how they handle situations, and incorporate that information in your own modus operandi where it's appropriate.

The Now Economy is all about being relevant. How do you know you're being relevant? Through very conscious effort, skill, and constant awareness of what's going on around you and how each shift in your external environment can create changes in your life.

You Are More Relaxed and More Comfortable With Yourself and Feel Less Defensive

By accumulating experiences of little and big successes, you'll eventually discover that you're no longer afraid. You have stood up to challenges and fears. And you have prevailed. Sure, maybe they all didn't turn out as you wanted, but even in these so-called failures you prevailed because you made it through and learned from the experience. This is a big part of becoming relaxed and comfortable. You know you can't be destroyed. You can be dinged and dented. You may even get fired. But your essential self and your fundamental sense of security will remain intact. Play even the worst possible hand bodaciously and you'll come out better for the experience.

You will feel less defensive and, as a result, less offensive. You'll be able to deflect uninvited criticisms, mind games, and even your own negative self-talk. The more bodacious you become, the more you realize that you don't have to prove yourself to others. Knowing that you have options and intrinsic value, you know you have more opportunities than the particular one immediately before you. You will stand your ground and assert your values more and more often. You will prove yourself in high-level ways, through your assertiveness rather than your eagerness to please.

Have you noticed that when you're feeling defensive or disempowered, you allow other people to call the shots? The hypercritical, pessimistic, or abusive people in your circle will talk in terms of the glass being half-empty, or maybe even shattered into sharp shards on the floor. And you're in there, with dustpan and broom, frantically sweeping up the mess. But when you're more relaxed and comfortable with yourself, you have control over the vocabulary you use to define your circumstances. When you hear "Know what I mean?" or "Don't you agree?" you can put that stake in the ground, own your view of the situation, and say, "Actually, this is how I see it." You value your opinion and are more relaxed to choose your view, no matter what people are saying all around you.

You Go From Survivor to Victor

We all go through times in our lives when it seems that it's all we can do to hang on. We want to become experts at thriving, not surviving. But that takes the courage of letting go of tried and true survival habits. This is a risky proposition, but it's the only way you'll be able to get anywhere. Say you have fallen overboard in a stormy sea. The only thing you see that can save you is a buoy within your reach. Naturally, you grab onto it. The question is: When will you be willing to let go? Too many people become experts of that buoy; they are experts in the art of survival. They know everything about it: its paint, the texture of its surface, the way it smells, the sound of its bell, the number of times its beacon flashes. But that won't get them anywhere. Holding on tight may help you personally and professionally for a while. But it's easy to forget that this is only a temporary solution. Eventually, you've got to let go, start swimming, and make progress again.

It's bodacious to let go of that buoy and throw yourself into a risky environment, at least risky compared to your survivor approach. But this is how you find success. Hanging on isn't good enough when you're bodacious. Neutral isn't good enough. Maintenance isn't good enough. Even though those positions may seem beneficial, they're really keeping you oriented toward fear and worst-case scenarios. Chances are that the worst case won't happen, and if it does, you manage it. When you're living the Bodacious Way you're spending most of your time focused on the positive aspects of living.

Issues will arise, and you will deal with them. But then you will immediately return to focusing on the joy of life rather than merely dedicating yourself to problem prevention.

You Give Yourself More Credit

When you give yourself credit, you reinforce in your own mind the systems, techniques, and methods that work for you. You identify and focus on the ways you can positively contribute to your career, your community, and your family. You notice and draw strength from all that's going right in your life and use part of that strength to deal with anything negative and to fuel personal growth.

In my early AOL days I always told new hires that the great part about working at AOL is that you get noticed and the worst part about working at AOL is that you get noticed. For many positions, only one person had a particular set of responsibilities, so if she performed well, she got recognized for her work. If she was a poor performer, it was equally noticeable, maybe more. I loved this environment because it allowed me to get credit for my contributions, and I was proud of my work. And when problems arose, I was motivated to find a solution. Remember, we're all start-ups, just as AOL was once. The steps we take and shifts we make—even the smallest ones—are noticeable. They have huge power to change our lives and our futures. Take time to notice those shifts and give yourself credit for having the courage to move forward with your vision for the future, regardless of what little emergencies or disappointments are crowding your immediate present.

You will also give yourself more credit at work. Looking at your career in new bodacious terms, you can easily identify exactly how your work contributes to the company's bottom line. Even if your job is traditionally considered a cost center, what you do helps the company make money. Figure out what that connection is. Talk and think about your work in those terms. And when you achieve objectives along those lines, let people know. Just as any company needs a public relations, marketing, or advertising function to position its products in the minds and hearts of its customers, you must do the same with your customer: your employer.

Giving yourself credit is not bragging, an accusation that every good girl avoids at all costs, including the cost of her own success and happiness. Giving yourself credit helps you recognize the internal shifts toward bodaciousness that you're achieving as an ongoing process of development. You're able to identify external accomplishments so you can package them in different ways and bring them to your marketplace as experiences and services that will make you more successful. Giving yourself credit helps you accept more graciously and naturally the credit other people give you. Giving yourself credit helps you become more fluent in giving other people credit as well. If you have the language to say positive and supportive things to yourself, you will be more genuine and effective in expressing supportive things to others.

And giving yourself credit is an excellent behavior to model to the women and girls in your life. You are giving yourself permission to shine brightly, and in doing so, you're letting others know that they can too.

You Do What It Takes to Create Your Best Physical, Emotional, and Mental Health

Christiane Northrup, author of *Women's Bodies, Women's Wisdom*, has this to say about the mind–body–spirit connection: "Our bodies are a wonderful barometer of how well we're living in the present and taking care of ourselves." As you develop in your bodaciousness, the way you choose to take care of yourself will show up as a healthier, more positive, and more energetic version of you.

A lot of books, videos, and classes are available to help you get in shape and feel good about yourself. I've certainly spent my share on them because I wanted the results they were promising. But, like many of us, I had limited success even with my most disciplined efforts. I still struggled with *wanting* to work so hard at trying to get my body to be the ideal image I had in my mind. What I didn't realize is that physical and emotional health is a manifestation of bodacious self-respect. Conversely, the slide out of fitness is a loud signal that there's something wrong.

For instance, before I was married I used to exercise, eat well, and feel pretty good about my body. But with the strains and challenges to my sense of self-esteem that my marriage created for me, my body and my happiness reflected my struggle. The week after I left my husband for the last time, I knew I wanted to get back to feeling terrific about my body and how I looked. Once I reclaimed my self-respect, it was amazing how easy it was to make the time to exercise. I was no longer fighting against myself.

It's not shallow to recognize that when you know you look better you feel better about yourself. You can see it as a vicious cycle. Or, if you're bodacious, you can see it as a beneficial cycle. The better you feel, the better you look; the better you look, the more likely you are to take care of your body, and that makes you feel even better.

Of course, the endorphins you get when you work out play a big part in this cycle. Nothing beats that elated, powerful feeling. Working out is also helpful in managing intense emotions, particularly anger, anxiety, and other toxic feelings.

Bodacious dreams take stamina in all facets of your existence: physical, mental, and emotional. By taking care of yourself, you are preparing one of the most important tools you need to realize your ambitions and act out the plans you have for your life. Ambition takes gumption, fortitude, and stamina. Fitness gives you the bodacious staying power you need.

You Are Constantly Learning

When you're bodacious, you will have an energized curiosity that will manifest itself in many different ways. You will seek out new ways of thinking and expose yourself to people and approaches that will broaden your own creativity and sense of what's possible in your life.

You will learn for the love of it. You will take classes, but you will also read more. You will strike up conversations with strangers. You will introduce yourself to coworkers throughout your organization, —not just in your department or on the same hierarchical level. You will see that bodacious learning is one of the most valuable ways to punch out the walls of your own self-assigned limitations, and you'll welcome every opportunity to discover the answers to questions you didn't even know existed.

You Are More Effective in Achieving Your Dreams

Bodacious women know what their dreams are, and they lay out an effective path to making them come true. Have you noticed how many people are more committed to the dream itself than to accomplishing that dream? These are the people who are always talking about "someday" or about their frustrations, anger, or irritation at repeatedly falling short of the mark. These are people who are in love with the *wish* rather than being fully committed to the *implementation*. Bodacious women operate in the realm of implementation.

For bodacious women, dreams aren't just wispy castles in the air. They are the end point to strategic planning. For bodacious women, goals are never beyond their reach. But they're well aware that they may have to stretch to get a solid hold on their objectives. Maybe they have to learn a new skill or a new language. Maybe they need to break the habits of certain self-definitions: They've been overweight all their lives, they can't save a penny, they're always negative or impatient, they never can make deadlines, or they don't have a head for math or computers. Bodacious women know that there are steps from here to there and that those steps can be discovered.

When you're living the bodacious life, you will think more strategically. You'll still dream, you'll still have big goals. The difference is that you'll also figure out how to get there and make your choices consistent with those goals. You will set timelines, and you will gather an advisory board to give you the expertise you don't already have. You will bodaciously evaluate each opportunity to choose in terms of "yes," "no," or "modify." If the choice is contrary to your values, objectives, or timeline, "no" is a very easy decision to make.

You Will Gain New Friends and Lose Others

You will attract and be attracted to other bodacious men and women. But you'll also find that the nonbodacious relationships you've had in the past will slide off your life as you progress.

The changes you make in your own life will affect others. Some will be inspired by your example and join the fun of this new way of living. Others will feel threatened, even betrayed or abandoned by your decision to leave your old ways and unproductive pain behind. Old relationships that can't support your personal growth will disappear. You will be breaking old covenants with people who thought they had power over you. Dominating parents, spouse, boss, or well-meaning friends may take it personally that you're rejecting their ways and values for new choices. They may tell you that you're being pushy, "full of yourself," or disrespectful, or that you're heading for trouble. They're reacting to the shock of a changing you. And they may actually disapprove of that change. That's their choice, but it doesn't have to be yours. It's time to sincerely wish them well and then move on.

During my last separation, which was clearly and publicly heading for divorce, a friend called one evening in a slightly nervous voice. After a short greeting she told me she couldn't continue to spend time with me because divorce was against her religious beliefs. I wasn't surprised because in the past few weeks I had sensed she was acting less and less comfortable whenever we were together. I knew she struggled to understand the choices I was making, and I knew that we still cared for each other. To this day, I'm grateful for her friendship and the support she did give me when I needed it the most. But now I was choosing a path that conflicted with her most cherished values. She was struggling with this difficult and sad choice. And I respected her freedom to choose. I didn't try to convince her otherwise, and as I hung up the phone I let her go.

On the other hand, you may find yourself needing to sincerely apologize as you're changing. Bodaciousness takes practice. As you're learning new skills and new ways to communicate your desires, you will probably be clumsy now and then. You may inadvertently hurt someone's feelings or let someone down. Change is messy; growth can be even messier. Give yourself room to try new skills. And be ready to apologize and sympathize with your cherished friends and family when you cause them unintended emotional pain.

You Will Take More Risks

Growth and ongoing development require you to constantly step into new territory and try new skills. That's a risky proposition! The real mark of the Bodacious Woman and the bodacious life is that both are filled with gutsy moves. I'm not talking about reckless risks. I'm suggesting that you ease into a gutsy life by trying on fun, smaller challenges and working outward from there. It could be something as simple as trying new restaurants and ordering something unfamiliar off a menu. Then talking to a stranger sitting next to you on the plane. Then spending a weekend or day just with yourself, maybe even vacationing alone. Then making it clear to your manager that you want to go to a conference in your area of expertise. Then making a speech. Then applying for and taking a job within a completely different department or company. Gently putting yourself into new situations. Gently expanding your tolerance for that feeling of "yikes!"

Saying "no" is also a risk. But always saying "yes" is unproductive when it's nonstrategic. If "yes" doesn't bring you closer to your dreams, your only alternative is "no." So give yourself credit for drawing boundaries. And don't feel you have to overexplain, or even explain your reason for saying no at all! If that's difficult for you, practice saying "no" and then offering alternatives to the person's request: "No, I can't do it now, but I can do it tomorrow." Eventually you'll be able to take the risk of saying a flat "no." Start with the telemarketers who interrupt your dinner.

You Will Help Other People Make Their Dreams Come True

The more powerful you become in your bodaciousness, the more you will be able to share that power with others and help their dreams come true. Through a more planful, strategic networking process, you will make friends with people who can make things happen. Then you will be the conduit to bring two or more needs together and create a dream out of that match. You will be more relaxed and creative, which puts you in the frame of mind to be receptive to strokes of genius and great ideas.

You will have a greater faith that there's plenty to go around. As a result you'll be more generous with your ideas, your acquaintances, and your encouragement. You will continue to pass on this new energy and help expand this whole Bodacious Way into the culture of both men and women.

You Will Break the Rules

When I was a child I was very compliant; I followed all the rules and respected authority and leadership. Or at least they easily intimidated me so I was afraid to step out of line. And rules served me well as a little girl. They protected me and taught me discipline at a time when I was developing into an adult who was expected to take care of herself. But now, as an adult, I look at rules differently. Instead of simply knowing what they are and dutifully following them, I consider their intent and decide whether they serve my intention. Living the Bodacious Way, I find myself following rules sometimes and breaking them other times.

What are the rules anyway, and who came up with them? It seems that so many rules aren't real rules at all, just common norms of behavior that fall into the category of "everyone does it that way." Worse, other rules tell you to play small, wait until everyone has stopped speaking before you open your mouth, wait to be acknowledged or called upon, or take what you've been given and be grateful for it. Those kinds of rules are set up to benefit others, not you. The universe is not going to smack you just because you leave the shopping cart in the middle of the parking lot, press the call bell for the flight attendant, take the biggest piece, change your assigned seat to a more comfortable one after the plane has taken off or the performance has begun, request a better table at a restaurant, ask for a discount, or use one job offer to leverage an improved offer from a competitor. You *can* do these things.

You Will Tell People What You Want

The most bodacious women I know are clear about what they want and are comfortable with saying so. They're not arrogant, they simply believe they're completely responsible for deciding who they want to be and what they need to do to get there. Sure, they seek input, but they know they're the only ones who can live their lives. Bodacious women also know how to tell others what they want at work, with friends, with family, with their spouse or significant other, and even themselves. They often use two simple, powerful words: "I need." The expanded mental version goes something like this: "I've decided I want to achieve this, so I need that and I'm telling you so. It's your choice; will you help me?" Often kindly, often enthusiastically, never sheepishly. "I need to obtain different perspectives about whether we should increase our product prices. I'd like your input. If you want to contribute, I need your thoughts by this Wednesday." You may get a better table in a restaurant, a discount, a raise four months ahead of schedule, or a promotion. Or maybe you won't. But you definitely won't if you don't tell people what you want.

I clearly remember one time when I made it clear to my manager what I needed. It was after I forgot my pants. Although I laughed at myself for looking more like I was ready to work out than have a business meeting, I knew something in my life had to give. This time it was my job. A week or so later, I told my boss, "I need to reduce my load so I can best handle grad school. I want to go part-time. Do you think that's possible?" In a few days I had my answer: "yes." I got what I wanted! But I never would have had I not made it known.

You Will Control Yourself, Influence Others, and Let the Rest Unfold

As a Bodacious Woman you will know that somewhere between controlling everything and being out of control is the most realistic place to be. Your life will be a mixture of proactively controlling what you can (yourself); influencing others through your relationships, your example, and your actions; and accepting the natural unfolding of events. Whatever the situation, you will confidently know that you always have the ability to control your response.

Bodacious women know that even the most airtight, contingency-proof strategy is subject to ongoing tweaks and adjustments. Still, there will be disappointments, maybe even tragedy. Bodacious women aren't exempt. But along the Bodacious Way you will notice the delights, large and small, the good fortunes, the surprises, the boosts, the synchronistic meeting of just the right people who can help each other in just the right way.

* * *

The purpose of this chapter is to give you a picture of what your life will look like and what you have to look forward to as a Bodacious Woman. Keep that picture in mind as you break through to bodaciousness so you know you're making progress and so you can keep on going even when the transition is uncomfortable. It's a wonderful ride on the Bodacious Way, but as with any journey, you will need a plan to fully bring it on. That comes next.

Bring It On!

IN THE LAST seven chapters you've been learning and, I hope, already using the skills, techniques, and attitudes that make up the Bodacious Way. In fact, you might already have some stories of micro-wins and successes as you have taken on touchy situations with that bigger and better version of yourself. I call those Bo Mos: Bodacious Moments.*

Taken one by one, all these techniques have started to change your life one isolated situation at a time,

---

*By now you probably have started experiencing some Bo Mos of your own. Please e-mail them to me via www.gobodacious. com, and I'll post the most bodacious ones as I get them. That way, other bodacious women will be inspired by your personal progress. There are some bodacious stories online already! Check it out and see for yourself!

in little, almost imperceptible ways, or maybe even in big, life-changing ways. If you've been using this book as you've been reading through the chapters, at least one person in your life is just dying to ask, "What has gotten *into* you?" At the very least, it's my wish that you have begun to develop a more calm, confident, proactive, even systematic approach to all areas of your life, even the ones that have long been especially troublesome or emotionally charged for you. You know the ones I'm talking about, don't you? The lessons that keep coming up again and again in your life in different disguises. An emotional button that a parent always manages to find and push. A promotion opportunity that keeps passing you over. That feeling that you're losing some political battle that you didn't even know you were fighting in the first place. The same point in every confrontational situation where you always back down, when you wish you had more staying power. The same bag of chocolate or popcorn you reach for when you're under extraordinary pressure, knowing full well that the only true effect it has in your life is going to show up on the scale.

Right. Time to move along. Time to bring it on! The future, that is. Now it's time to use the Bodacious Way to strategically create a future that's satisfying, creative, rewarding (both emotionally and financially), and not only is responsive to the changing times of the Now Economy but actually drives the way those changes positively affect your life. If you've been paying attention so far, you're ready. Remember how I said earlier that we're all start-ups? By using the techniques I'll describe in this chapter, you'll be benefiting from an actual business process that all start-ups need to do in mapping out their path: the business plan. This is a step-by-step action program that takes start-ups from *cool idea* to money in the bank and product on the store shelf. In this chapter I'm going to outline that valuable process and create a personal business plan, a tool that will take you farther than perhaps anything you have done so far in planning your life. This will be your personal step-by-step strategic action plan that will take you from your own personal dream to realization.

This chapter will guide you through the best project of all, creating a bodacious life on a macro level, in addition to all those wonderful wins of standing your ground and asserting your empowered, creative self. "Uh oh," I hear you saying, "here comes the bit about personal mission statements."

If you have this book, you probably already have at least one other book on your shelf that talks about personal mission statements. You've probably read Stephen Covey's *The 7 Habits of Highly Effective People* at least once. If you did the work in the book, then you don't need me to tell you how to put together a personal mission statement. If you didn't do the work in the book, then you're like Martha, who over the years has managed to buy at least seven copies of the book (one copy for each habit!) but wouldn't be caught dead actually doing the exercises. So you don't need me to tell you to pick up that pen and start journaling. You will or you won't. You'll help yourself if you do, and I heartily recommend it. (And there will be a point later in this chapter where you will need to clarify for yourself what your values, objectives, and personal mission are. But all in good time.)

Remember, we've already established that being bodacious is deciding who you want to be and then creating that new life for yourself. The next question, of course, is what do you do to make that happen. The problem with many of these personal growth books is that they don't take you far enough in the process. They get you inspired, maybe even fired up with a specific vision of the first part of the process: who you want to be. But they often leave you there, with no practical ideas on how to go about creating those changes. How many times have you said to friends (or have they said to you), "I know what I want to do, but I just have no idea how to go about getting there, step-by-step"? If we stopped our exploration at the personal mission statement stage without installing an actual plan to alter our lives accordingly, our great new intentions are left vulnerable to those same destructive emotional habits and negative mental tapes that have been playing in our heads for so long. Our future is left in the hands of our self-esteem (which, as we all know, isn't the most stable and consistent custodian). And the daily decisions we make are again governed by our emotional state, most notably our fears, insecurities, and doubts.

This is your inner voice trying to make a major life change based on mission statement alone: "Well, gee, I don't know. I was all charged up last week about going after being chosen as the project head for the new product launch. But I feel kind of fat this morning. Do my cheeks look puffy to you? And I'm still getting over my hurt feelings from yesterday. If I tried to look bodacious today, everyone would know I'm bluffing. I mean, who am I kidding? I would look like such a phony trying to pull something off today. I think I'll wait until tomorrow to get bodacious. Maybe I'll feel better about myself then."

This is your inner voice building a change according to your personal business plan: "Okay, here's the plan: Get in the car. Go to work. Make that call to John, who's selecting the project lead; I'll probably get voice mail anyway. I can keep up the bodacious energy in the short time it takes to leave a message. Get this month's expense report finished. See if Sharon can join me for lunch; she's always motivating. Call my personal coach for a quick shot of renewed purpose. Reread the chapter on taking a stand before going into the meeting this afternoon. Go to the gym after work. At the club meeting tonight, introduce myself to one new person according to the plan. Drink a cup of chamomile tea before going to bed tonight, and read something pleasant in bed instead of watching television."

Step by step. It's not about how you're feeling about yourself from one moment to the next. It's not even about how you're feeling about the activity on the plan. It's about straightforwardly following the blueprint you've chosen for your life, a blueprint that's available to you regardless of what you ate last night, who snubbed you this morning, or whether you signed up to run a charity race next weekend. The personal business plan takes you above the choppy surface of your moods and fluctuating self-esteem. It gives you a stable, steady structure to follow, a structure you have been building in a calm and thoughtful time, so you know that you will be able to trust it in the not-so-calm-and-thoughtful times.

For companies, the business plan is what defines their vision in real and measurable objectives, attracts millions of dollars in investment capital, protects the companies from being distracted by nonessential activities, and helps them identify the assets, skills, and talent they need to acquire and the steps they need to take to meet their objectives. Unless you aspire to be the next Martha Stewart (talk about Bodacious Woman!), you probably don't have "multimedia billionaire mogul" in your personal business plan. So millions of dollars in investment capital probably won't be a priority for you, but maybe a recession-proof retirement fund is.

Here are some other objectives that might be in your personal business plan:

* An assignment working and living abroad, maybe even someplace specific (say China? France? Australia?)

* A more promising career track with an income that matches the value of your contributions

* A serene, positive, supportive home life

* A graduate degree

* A leadership role in your profession

* A twenty-five-pound weight loss

* A schedule that gives you time to pursue your passions while being the primary caretaker of an aging parent

* Children who are healthy, safe, and optimistic about their future

These are all objectives—actual, visible, measurable facts of a life—that you can realize for yourself by following a fully fleshed out personal business plan.

What We Can Learn From New Economy Business Mistakes

Over the next several years, plenty of comprehensive articles and books will be written about the New Economy and its disappointments. But the New Economy holds a couple of valuable lessons for us as we build our Now Economy lives.

MISTAKE 1: THE FLIP FLOPPED

In his prophetic article "Built to Flip" in the March 2000 issue of *Fast Company* magazine (exactly one month before the infamous April NASDAQ meltdown), Jim Collins, coauthor of *Built to Last*, wrote that greed—indeed, *fast* greed—had become the driving purpose of start-ups launched in the New Economy. "Today it's enough to pull together a good story, to implement the rough draft of an idea and—presto!—instant wealth."

But where did that instant wealth come from? From investors who expected a return on their investment (ROI), and pretty darn quick. Suddenly any lofty vision for changing the world—or even the marketplace—took back seat to profits. When the profit motive starts driving the enterprise, impatience sets in. The lack of faith sets in. Then dreams begin to dull and tarnish. Then pink slips fly. By the end of 2000, more than 41,000 employees of what had promised to be the most exciting market sector in a long time had lost their jobs. Along with holiday segments about worried retailers facing empty stores because of the unusually severe weather skating across the country in December, there was weepy footage of one dot.com after another counting down to offline.

These countdowns marked more than just the end of the delightfully annoying pets.com sock puppet or those fabulously decadent and diva-esque spokesflowers for garden.com (some of the best television in the late 1990s were in the commercials, born of dot.coms' gigantic advertising budgets). They marked the end of the visions of both the entrepreneurs and the impassioned people working for them. But for many of their capital investors, these were bloodless losses. They just wrote off the disappointments and moved along.

By June 2001, over a half million layoffs were announced across all industries, including much-admired Cisco Systems.

In the built-to-flip environment that the New Economy devolved into, the loudest, most demanding customer was also the most ruthless. Don't perform fast enough for acceptable ROI, and the plug is pulled. And all the values with the most staying power—dreams, passion, vision—get swirled.

In contrast, the Old Economy built-to-last model that Collins describes in his best-selling book recognizes a longer time line, one that sustains a balance of preserving the core and stimulating progress. The Old Economy companies that serve as exemplars of Collins's idea of excellence and permanence allowed plenty of shift and transformation while staying true to some fundamental principles that guided most of their decision making. And when those principles were in conflict with pressure of outside market influences (such as the big investors), these built-to-last companies were better able and willing to stand by the principles. Result: No countdown for these companies.

As we build our Bodacious Way personal business plan, it's best to follow more closely the example and inspiration of built-to-last companies rather than the New Economy built-to-flip model. Built-to-flip thinking puts us in perpetual survival mode, where we're constantly resolving crises and responding to short-term demands rather than sacrificing a little bit now to achieve long-term, more permanent objectives that will add the most value. Sure, the Now Economy has a different market dynamic than the Old Economy, but dismissing the practices that worked and worked well just isn't smart.

By building our personal business plan to last, we are designing for ourselves a program that keeps us steadily heading in the direction of our dreams and values. But we're also building in resilience, flexibility, and responsiveness to all the external factors that will crop up along the way.

With a personal business plan that's built to last, our vision and principles are the customers we must please. This isn't to say that the decisions and choices we make will be any easier. But they will result in long-term ROI that we can not only live with but thrive by.

MISTAKE 2: PLANNING IS FOR WIMPS

New Economy start-ups were perpetually under pressure by their investors to hit the market long before their vision was fully transformed into a must-have product or service. Because of the growing competition—the very real possibility that someone had the exact same idea the night before you did—that pressure for speed started showing up earlier and earlier in the development process, almost making you feel that if you waited to change out of your pajamas before sharing your brainstorm with a possible investor, you'd already be too late. The guy in his jammies from the night before might have already beaten you to the punch and eaten your lunch. And sometimes that was indeed the case. That's one of the mysteries of being human in the modern, creative era: How can a single stroke of brilliance lie undiscovered throughout the world for two millennia only to show up in the dreams of five different go-getters in Silicon Valley in the space of forty-eight hours?

So in many corners of the New Economy start-up game, the business plan phase was skipped altogether. It was enough, as Collins pointed out, to have a good story and a rough draft of an idea. In fact, actually having a formal, fully developed business plan positioned you for getting laughed out of an investor's meeting as being hopelessly behind the times. Only a Luddite would invest so much upfront time on an actual proposal. Remember the guy in the jammies? He's already broken out the champagne, paid for with the first check from his investors.

Well, as the NASDAQ market has shown, some of those Old Economy ways might not have been such a bad idea after all. Of course, not all New Economy companies tried to fly without a business plan, but many did. And many don't exist anymore. As the old expression goes, "Fail to plan and you plan to fail." At least you can plan to morph into something you never would have intended. One of Martha's Silicon Valley contacts explained what had happened to his company that started out offering Web-based services to company employees:

> Last year we completely changed our name and logo. This year we left the Internet space altogether, and have started developing and selling packaged software instead serving an entirely different market segment.

Call back in a couple of months, he told her. "By that time we'll probably will have turned into a rental car agency."

Being a rental car agency is great—assuming that that was the plan all along.

By ditching the plan process (Mistake 2), New Economy companies put themselves at risk for being hurt even more when they start making Mistake 1. And that trap is so much easier to fall into when you don't know who you are and what future you have committed yourself to.

So now in the post–New Economy era, we're all in the same boat: semiconductor companies, soap companies, you, and me. Whether we made a million or we just barely made the rent, we share the same bodacious Now Economy opportunity: To take what we've learned from the past and start up again.

One thing we now know for sure: To make any bodacious dream stick, we need to start with a bodacious plan, a plan that grows as we grow, allows for creative change and helps us anticipate change before it happens to us, and gives us a stable framework to respond to unpredicted change in ways that don't take us in unwanted directions.

Because we're all start-ups, I've decided to borrow the basic business plan model and create a structure that you'll have fun following, designing for yourself the step-by-step program that will walk you through your future, authentic, bigger and bolder self.

(And one of the best parts of the personal business plan is that it has built-in milestones to celebrate. The accomplishment is a virtue unto itself, but nothing is more motivating than a big, fun bash, especially one that follows great news. Steve Case doesn't throw all those great parties just because he has a stash of paper plates in his basement.)

Your Big, Bodacious Personal Business Plan

Creating a personal business plan may sound odd and over-the-top. But it's useful and practical, and it gives you a strategic platform on which to build your dream (and you certainly know by now that strategy is the name of the game). As with a business, the main purpose here is to make yourself more effective and more efficient with your time and resources and to build a more powerful personal competitive advantage. By laying out all the details, you reduce your risk of failure and increase your chances for success. You even anticipate the potential difficulties, which will help you respond more effectively because you thought through those responses beforehand, while you were clear-headed and calm. Think of the confidence that alone will inspire!

Your personal business plan can walk you through an entire life or career makeover. Or maybe you basically like your life and what you do, and you just want to move up a notch (whatever "up" means to you). This plan will work for you if you take yourself seriously enough to think of yourself as a business. Generally speaking, companies (whether they are start-up or long-term Old Economy companies) review their plans at least once a year, making sure their strategies are still legitimate in the business environment, that their actions are still consistent with their vision, and that they haven't left any valuable part of their enterprise neglected.

Are you your own business? You are if you are a Bodacious Woman in the Now Economy! So let's get started engineering the Now Economy You Version 2.0.

STEP 1: YOU ARE HERE

There are three main parts of any business plan:

Step 1: The current state of your situation

Step 2: What you want your desired future to look like

Step 3: What you have to do to get there

So here we are at Step 1. In the business circles, it has been called the strategic analysis step, which sounds about as exciting as filling out tax forms. So let's just call it the You Are Here step; or simply Step 1 for short.

One advantage of Step 1 is that it helps you understand as thoroughly as possible your current situation. And it guides you through the process of discovering what you like as much as it helps you identify the circumstances you want to change. Haven't you noticed that when you're driven to make a change, you're so focused on the sources of your unhappiness that you overlook the areas that give you true satisfaction? You can learn as much from uncovering what brings you satisfaction—perhaps even more, because satisfaction is your goal—than you can by focusing only on what brings you pain. Which would you rather be an expert in?

As I've said, the personal business plan can be applied to almost any aspect of your life. This same business plan model can be overlaid onto any area that concerns you, from something as trivial as learning how to knit Icelandic sweaters, to building more rewarding family relationships, to something as traumatic and life-altering as leaving a painful marriage and creating a new life where you can feel safe and happy. It may seem ridiculous to apply the same principles to such widely diverse interests and concerns. But this is the beauty of the personal business plan. It allows you to take a much-needed break from the charged emotionalism of the challenge before you, pleasant or unpleasant, and strategically plot your steps to a better future. For simplicity's sake, I'm going to focus on your career to demonstrate how the personal business plan works.

Here are the essential parts of Step 1 as it would apply to your career.

Career Overview

What is your current job's purpose? How do you measure your effectiveness? Are you satisfied with your effectiveness? Are you allowed to perform your duties to your satisfaction without demoralizing treatment or too many distracting interruptions? What are you doing now that you weren't doing one or two years before? What new skills have you learned? Do those changes represent a satisfactory rate of growth for you? Does the job still hold meaning for you? Does it embody your most cherished values, principles, and beliefs? Can you identify ways in which your job responds to the most important values in your life? Are you physically located in a community that supports your outside interests, passions, and values? Is your income satisfactory? Are you paid the salary you know you're worth—at least commensurate with similar positions in your market, with enough to live a comfortable life, to do the things you want, while being able to plan for the future in all its aspects (your children's education and your own retirement, for instance)? Is the reason why you once said "yes" to the job offer still compelling enough to keep you going to work?

What parts of your current job do you enjoy and would want to take with you as your career progresses? What other aspects of your work leave you fatigued or burned out? What tasks make time fly for you? What other tasks cause the day to creep by? Do you have a way to delegate those tasks?

Do you enjoy your profession but wish you could apply it in a different industry? Or do you like the industry you're in but are ready to change or expand your role in it? Do you love the industry but are ready to change companies within it? Or would you like to just chuck it all and start all over again?

Make a list of both the positive and negative emotions that you associate with your current career (or, if this isn't a career personal business plan, whatever area of your life that you're creating this plan for). Creative satisfaction? Frustration? Guilt? Gratitude? Fascination? Anger? Exuberance? Exhaustion? Don't get mired down in those feelings, as if they color your entire experience. Take an objective step back from those feelings and use them as diagnostic tools. Notice the feeling and objectively consider *why* you're feeling that way. Then ask why again, and again, until you've got your real answer. What do the *whys* tell you about what elements you should carry with you into your future and which ones you can leave behind?

Company Overview

What is the company's mission and values? Can you support them? Does the company make a product or a service that you are proud of? Does it have a culture that invigorates you, or do you dread walking through the front doors every day? Do you work for a company or industry that supports and encourages your development (not just talk but support you actually experience in the form of training, projects, conferences, and promotions)? Does it support corporate citizenship values that are meaningful to you, such as flexibility for family demands, community outreach, environmental awareness, or diversity considerations? Does it insist that the workplace is a safety-conscious abuse-free zone that holds a zero-tolerance policy for not only drugs but also harassment and other demeaning behavior?

Who are your employer's competitors? What is the state of their viability in the marketplace? Are they financially sound? Are they a distant second to your own company's? Are they worthy competitors, perhaps employers to consider as an alternative to your own company? Or does your company still offer the best career advantages and prestige? Are there new entries into your company's market space that might be easy to overlook now but could be serious contenders in the near future? (Remember, in its earliest days AOL was dismissed as a distant third upstart behind the far more established CompuServe and Prodigy.)

An excellent source for identifying your company's closest competitors (especially if you work for a large national corporation) is www.hoovers.com. This site not only lists the main competitors for any publicly traded company but also provides descriptions of their competitive positioning, names of key officers and executives, and hyperlinks to their Web sites so you can explore the job opportunities there directly.

Speaking of competitors, who may be a competitor for your current job? Who is positioned right behind you to naturally and logically assume your responsibilities as you move forward? If your company is about to undergo a merger or acquisition, who is your counterpart at the other company? Will there be room for only one of you once the deal is completed?

For that matter, who preceded you in your current position? The more recent the transition, the more powerful that competition is, even if it's only in the form of the Ghost of the Old Way. If you are frequently reminded of "how it used to be done," like it or not, one of your competitors is someone who has moved on. If that person is still with the company, especially the same building, the gravitational pull of nostalgia can undermine your effectiveness and dilute your power until enough time has passed, or you accomplish any extraordinary objective, to lay that particular ghost to rest.

Market Overview

In your role, who are your customers, both internal and external? (Even if you have an internal position that doesn't interact directly with your company's customers, you still have someone to please in your role; who is it?) How satisfied are they? Are you proud to be associated with them? Do they agree with you as to how value, quality, and success are defined? Is everyone equally invested in the success of your shared objectives? Or do you run up against differing priorities?

What part do you play in getting the end result to the customer? Who buys from you? Who sells to you? Would you like to take their place? What business are you really in?

If you can name only one kind of customer, think some more. Let's say you work for Polaroid in the public relations department. You could reasonably say, "I work in the photography industry, and my customer is the family that wants the instant gratification of high-quality pictures in a matter of seconds."

But you could also say, "I work in communications, and my customer is the company that wants a positive reputation among its buyers, investors, and other business relationships."

You could also say, "I support the news media, and my customers are the journalists who depend on me for the accurate information and access they need to do their work."

You could also say, "I'm a professional responsible for the success of a major employer in New England. How I position the company in the public eye affects the job security for thousands of people throughout a small region that has suffered some hard times economically. So my customers are not only Polaroid's employees but also the cities and villages where they live and purchase goods and services."

You could also say, "My calling is to be in public relations, and it doesn't matter what company I work for. My mission is to do a good job in PR and promote the value of the profession to corporate America."

Or you could say, "My calling is to provide a secure home for my family and a good role model for my children.

See? Here are six links already that can attach to your value mesh. You can follow any one of those links to a rewarding career future, depending on which one (or ones) appeal to your personal vision the most compellingly.

When considering your market overview, you should also identify the externalities—market conditions that you can't do anything about—that will affect the overall vitality of your industry or profession. Now that you've stopped to look, can you see the writing on the wall that tells you that within five years your skills or contributions may no longer be in demand marketwide? Is your company about to hit a huge public relations hailstorm, and will the pummeling it will get show up in decreased market share in the stores? (Obviously, if you were a PR professional, as in our example, this particular externality could spell a terrific opportunity for you to demonstrate that you perform well in a crisis.)

STEP 2: YOU WILL BE HERE

This is the step in which you create the vision of the future you want for yourself. In creating a major change that's built to last, you will be working on two levels in this step: identifying your enduring values and understanding how those values might be man-ifested in different ways as external conditions change. Remember, as a Bodacious Woman, the prospect of shift and change is an excit-ing one, not a threatening one. That's because you've come to relate to the world as a visionary company, which "distinguishes its time-less core values and enduring purpose (which should never change) from its operating practices and business strategy (which should be changing constantly in response to a changing world)," as Collins says in *Built to Last*.

In the typical business plan, this is the envisioned solution to a problem (or business opportunity) after all the steps have been made and the parts are in place (which we'll cover in Step 3). All the com-ponents of Step 2 describe the future vision as if it has already hap-pened. When it comes to determining who you want to be as an individual (remember, in this example, we're using your career as the aspect to focus on at the moment), the process is similar. All the components of Step 2 should help you paint the overall picture that answers the question, "Who do I want to become?"

Here are some of the components of the standard business plan that help companies arrive at that answer. Because we're all start-ups, they will help you envision your future as well:

* *Your personal values, mission and objectives.* How will your future career look and feel? What will it be like going to work every morning? How will you experience workday happiness? Will the environment be supportive and respectful? Will you be able to dedicate the necessary time to be with your children at important school and extracur-ricular events? Will you be in Paris or Mozambique? Will you be able to save aggressively and invest wisely for your future? Do you want more creative independence? Do you prefer the fun and risk of working for a start-up, for less money but more stock options, with the idea that you might eventually be positioned to cash in? Do you want to work in a less demanding environment so you can reserve

some of your emotional and mental energies for other high-pressure aspects of your life, such as grad school or volunteer work?

This is the point where it's valuable to invest a lot of time and concentration to examine exactly what's in your heart and bursting to assert itself in the way you enjoy life. This particular stage is too big to try to incorporate into a single chapter of a larger book. But there are plenty of excellent books to guide you through this one step. Among our favorites are *I Could Do Anything if I Only Knew What It Was* and *Live the Life You Love*, two books by Barbara Sher, and *The Path* by Laurie Beth Jones.

* *Critical success factors.* What needs to be in place for your success to happen? A supervisor who supports your growth? A company where upward mobility for women is welcomed? A corporate policy that's family friendly? Fellow employees who share your vision and don't mind making necessary sacrifices to make it happen? Do you need to move to a larger city? Is the necessary technology easily available to you? Do you need to acquire more skills? Do you need to meet some influential people and cultivate their political support? If you're the sole financial support for your home, how dependable must your income be so that you can allow yourself to focus on your vision? What kind of external support can you retain to free yourself up even more? Author Barbara Sher, for instance, urges the women in her workshops to retain housekeeping help as soon as they can afford it, even if that help is once a month. This is a necessity, not an indulgence, says Sher, herself once a struggling single mother living hand to mouth. Not only does it free you up from chores that offer little or no long-term return on your investment but it also provides badly needed income for other women who are struggling to make ends meet.

* *Entry barriers.* The environment you will work in must be able to support this new version of yourself. What does this mean in practical terms? Do you have to quit your company altogether, or can you do what I did: transition into a part-time job or one with less pressure? If that is impossible with your current employer, that would be called an entry barrier: a characteristic of the business environment that would keep you from realizing your dream. Other entry barriers might be lack of demand in the marketplace for Now Economy You Version 2.0. Or you might lack support at home—financial or emotional—that you would need to get through the rough transition period. Or you might need a huge infusion of cash to make the transition, and only you believe that the commitment will be worth it.

* *Future iterations of your vision.* Although your values probably will never change, the way those values show up in your career are bound to change over the course of your working life. For instance, perhaps right now your values are to deliver world-class professionalism on the job and be a supportive, always available parent. Perhaps you discover for yourself (I'm not taking a position here; this is just an example) that you can't do both full-time. So while the children are young, you are able to realize your vision of working drastically reduced hours. As the children mature and become more independent, you are able to increase your hours on the job. By the time they leave home for college, you are fully employed at work again, delivering the world-class professionalism that is an integral part of your values.

  That ability to respect and respond to your values, all the while shifting the balance between work and home as the market allows (even demands), is an example of sustained competitive advantage, a loaded-sounding business term that really just means how are you going to continue to be valuable in the marketplace.

In the next step we'll go into greater detail about the strategies you can use, but for now it's important for you to understand that as you envision your future, in all its rich detail, the ability of that future to continue being successful depends largely on your ability to morph your behaviors, taking on new skills, or core competencies, as the external circumstances dictate. Being changeable in this way is a sign of strength and dedication to the things that are the most meaningful to you in life.

Eleven Ways to Make Your Own Luck

Good luck in the Now Economy is a chemical reaction of relationships: the relationships you have with other mission-driven people, the relationship you have with your profession, the relationship you have with the world, and the relationship you have with yourself.

1. **KNOW WHAT YOU WANT.** What does good luck mean to you? A career that's fascinating and meaningful? The ability to make a significant difference in a cause that's important to you? Corporate stature and power? A certain amount of money? A career that will let you work at home? A position that sends you to Beijing? When you know exactly what good luck looks like to you, you'll be able to focus on ways to get there.

2. **DECLARE YOUR SPIRIT A FUNK-FREE ZONE.** A positive mental and emotional outlook helps you attract life-changing opportunities and relationships. Cultivate hopeful, optimistic, and inspiring friends; celebrate their achievements; focus on what's going well in your own life. Eliminate relationships that are negative or abusive. Likewise, erase critical self-talk mental tapes you play in your own mind. If you feel guilty or badly about a specific aspect of your life, deal

with it according to your conscience and get on with the joy of being alive. Get professional help for chronic anxiety or depression. Remember that fun activities are an important part of your mental health. They make you happy and they put you in situations where you meet other happy people.

3. **CORRECT THE DETAILS THAT HOLD YOU BACK.** You are not your flaws, but sometimes it feels that way, especially when your confidence is low. Fix the things you can: Lose or gain weight, straighten or whiten your teeth, retain a personal shopper to help you upgrade your wardrobe, improve your nutrition and fitness program, or take a course in business writing, etiquette, or diction. Whatever it is that worries you, there is probably a solution for it. You can find it. Your goal is not to be perfect; your goal is to be confident.

4. **COUNT YOUR BLESSINGS.** We already know the importance of gratitude for what we receive. But we should also remember the many ways we bless others. Are you a generous advisor, spending a lot of time supporting friends in transition? Does your own example inspire courage, hope, creativity, resourcefulness, or laughter among your friends? All those benefits are an important part of your brand that you can capitalize on to give you access to powerful people and opportunities.

5. **UNDERSTAND THE GREATER CONTEXT OF YOUR CAREER.** Now Economy jobs are absorbing and demanding. Most of the time it will feel as though it's more than you can do to stay on top of your to-do list. But make sure you keep a big-picture perspective on how your work fits into the larger puzzle of your department, your company, your local economy, your profession, your industry, and your life.

6. REACH UP TO AT LEAST ONE NEW SENIOR PERSON EACH MONTH. Use that big-picture perspective to identify at least one new person to introduce yourself to every four weeks or so. You have no purpose other than to know and get known in as many areas of your work as possible. Initiate a meeting with someone accessible, perhaps someone within your company. Simply share something you admire about them and say that you'd like to get to know them better. If you can get a lunch meeting, great! If not, given their busy schedule, suggest a chat over a cup of coffee at the beginning of their day (you'll have less chance of being rescheduled or postponed). The last alternative is a phone conversation. No matter what, have at least two or three questions to ask and at least one thing you want them to know about you. If it goes well, explain your plan and ask for advice on who next to meet and permission to use his or her name when making first contact.

7. REACH DOWN TO AT LEAST ONE JUNIOR PERSON EACH MONTH. It's just as important to know powerful people behind you as it is to know powerful people ahead of you in your career. Whether you're beginning your career or more advanced, many people will benefit from your example and advice. And if they're currently in your organization, in the future they could get things done or provide information. Cultivate relationships with these valuable contacts. One day they could be your staff, your colleagues, or your competitors.

8. ACCEPT MORE INVITATIONS THAN YOU DECLINE. Take every opportunity to expand your social and business contacts. Every person you meet represents an opportunity to make a difference somewhere in your life or career or the world.

9. **LEARN FROM GREATNESS.** Read biographies of a wide variety of people (or watch them on television). Through their life stories, you'll get the long-view wisdom that success is not just about doing well day to day but about staying hopeful and true to your vision even during the bad times.

10. **GO PUBLIC.** Learn to love public speaking (or at least get very comfortable with it). Write and submit articles to your local newspaper or trade journal. Become an active volunteer with your local professional association and enter its leadership track. Participate frequently on relevant Internet listservs and cultivate one-on-one e-mail relationships with other active correspondents on the lists.

11. **EXPAND YOUR WORLD THROUGH READING.** Regularly read your local newspaper and a major national daily, such as *The New York Times.* If your career is particularly business-oriented, read *The Wall Street Journal.* Send congratulatory notes or e-mails to people whose stories are particularly interesting or inspiring to you.

STEP 3: WAY TO GO!

Now that you have been able to paint for yourself a detailed picture of your ideal future, it's time to plot a strategy for achieving that future. Remember, in this example we're just talking about your career, but this same plan can be applied to every aspect of your life. You didn't know you were a conglomerate, did you?

Step 3 is the difference between getting stuck in emotionalizing your dreams, feeling frustrated that they haven't already happened for you, and thinking negatively versus staying calm, confident, focused, patient, and productive. Step 3 is what helps you build a strategy to stay consistent with your vision while being flexible and resilient in the face of ever-changing times and shifting circumstances.

STRATEGY 1: MAKE SURE YOUR STEPS GET YOU WHERE YOU WANT TO GO

As Stephen Covey wrote in *The 7 Habits of Highly Effective People*, "Put first things first." Or, as I heard at a talk in college, "Keep the main thing the main thing." Outline exactly what steps tie directly to your vision and try not to stray from them—at least not very often. Distractions happen. Get quickly back on track.

Is this where you commonly get stuck? It's a common complaint: "If I knew what steps to take, I wouldn't be buying all these expensive how-to books!" Fair enough. So here's the first step to take: Get advice from people who have already achieved your mission. Call them or send them an e-mail, requesting an appointment, either on the phone or in person (in person is always the best option). The worst thing they can do is say "no." But unless you're talking movie stars or anyone else you might read about in *In Style* magazine, just about anyone will give you ten minutes. If in they see your sincerity and enthusiasm (and can be sure that you're not a stalker or out to get their job), those ten minutes can easily turn into a half hour, a list of more names to contact, and maybe even a job lead. Nothing opens doors faster than a good dose of sincere, smart, and thoughtful humanity. Almost everyone is "just folks" at heart.

The good news is this: Any information or piece of advice that you want about the path to making your vision a reality already exists. Someone knows the answer. And that someone probably will talk to you, at least for the ten minutes it takes to show that person that you're serious about achieving the same goal they're just dying to talk to someone about (after all, their family and friends already know the story, know the jokes, and know how it ended).

So maybe you don't know who these people are and how to get through to them. That's not so difficult as it may seem at first. Just remember that the answers are there somewhere. Here are just a few examples:

* Start leveraging the network you've been building using your bodacious relationship skills. Even if they aren't doing

what you're aiming for, it's very possible they can refer to someone in their network who's a great match.

* If you're committed to the profession and would like to meet your counterparts at other companies, you should consider membership with your professional association (which may have a local chapter convenient to you). If you don't know what that association (or associations) is and if asking around your business doesn't help, research the Web site for the American Society for Association Executives (www.asaenet.org).

* If you're looking for a personal coach to help get you started, you can find a directory of professional coaches at the International Coach Federation:
www.coachfederation.com

* Try fellow alumni from undergraduate or gradate school. Many colleges and universities have Web sites where you can search for alumni according to geographic area or degree. Also consider any clubs or groups you were involved in while in school that may have directories, such as sororities or academic groups.

* If it's a family or workplace diversity question that relates to the company you're already working in (and are devoted to), see whether your company has a women's leadership or support group.

* If you're looking for a new employer that has a terrific record for being good to its employees, check out *Fortune* magazine's annual "Best Companies to Work For" list. It's published every January, but you can access it year-round at www.fortune.com.

* If you're looking for companies with a good family-friendly track record, *Working Mother* magazine publishes an annual list. That list is available online via www.workingmother.com.

* Or perhaps where you're living takes precedence over what you do. You need to stay geographically put, but you still need a job you'll love. Go where the employers go! Most major metro areas have local chapters of the Society for Human Resource Management. Their members usually meet at least once a month for interesting lunch or dinner programs. It's a casual and relaxed way to get acquainted with your area's leading employers. Keep it dignified; this is the place to exchange business cards, not distribute résumés. This is not a job fair. They're there to stay current with their colleagues and trends in their profession. For a directory of local chapters near you, visit www.shrm.org.

* If you still need a little push and direction to get you started, contact Martha and me at www.gobodacious.com. One of us—maybe even both—will be happy to give you the best guidance we can.

Obviously it's impossible to list all the information opportunities there are for every conceivable goal you might have. This list was just to prove that the answers you're looking for are likely to be easily accessible.

Then your job is to map out to your satisfaction exactly what the steps are to arriving at your mission. You'll know what activities serve your mission. And you'll know which activities would only distract you and eat up valuable time. This to-do list will help you say no to the temptation list.

STRATEGY 2: UNDERSTAND HOW YOUR STRATEGIC BUSINESS UNITS RELATE TO EACH OTHER

Large companies often end up having a variety of operations that are so well developed, with their own well-defined markets, obligations, and even different sets of competitors, that they could easily be considered separate businesses. But they also compete with each other for the parent company's resources, time, and attention.

These are strategic business units, separate but still dependent on the mother ship. You have strategic business units as well: your children and their needs, your husband and his needs, your job and its needs, your ambition to launch your own company, your commitment to physical fitness, and your degree program. All the separate and compelling demands on your resources must be considered carefully.

As companies progress according to their business plans, they pause now and then to reconsider how their strategic business units have evolved with time and how their needs have changed. This helps the parent company reallocate resources to suit each unit's needs more appropriately and effectively. That reallocation may not necessarily be fair in the eyes of the individual business units, but given the consideration it deserves, the reallocation should always be responsive to the company's long-term vision.

Maybe the last time you gave all your strategic business units any serious planning consideration was when your youngest was still in diapers, your husband was losing a turf battle at work, and you needed to find a way to get to the gym sometime between the 5 A.M. feeding and the 8:30 conference call to Taiwan. Now your youngest has his driver's license and your husband has his own company. These two strategic business units are doing just fine; now you can focus your assets on bringing along your own bodacious vision.

The shifts of balance among all your own strategic business units over time—the addition of fresh dreams, an unexpected illness, new family members through marriage or adoption—all demand that you follow the business example and periodically review the interplay of the many aspects of your life. And give each unit the time and attention it needs to support and fulfill your vision.

STRATEGY 3: PREACH IT, SISTER!

Who needs to understand your dream? Potential investors in the new e-business plan you devised? Your kids, as you decide to sell the house and live aboard a forty-foot yacht in Pango Pango? Yourself, as you approach that twenty-five-pound goal?

Your vision may be lofty. It may be inspiring. It may save the world. Or maybe it'll just help the world get on the Internet faster. Maybe it will help you get into a size 8 dress. But it won't fly unless you're able to tell the story of your vision to your marketplace: your buyers, your employees, your investors, your community. Companies do this in a wide variety of ways, from producing commercials (some don't actually sell their product but sell the image of the company) to supporting the arts or education in their community, to cultivating relationships with journalists covering their industry, to sponsoring charity events. Many of these activities can be scaled down to meet almost any budget. In 2001, for instance, I sponsored a friend in her running events. For a very reasonable fee, I get a piece of her T-shirt to display my message on. What's my message? *Go bodacious!* What else?

Companies typically achieve their evangelizing objectives through their sales, marketing, and advertising departments. How you spread the message of your vision is limited only by your imagination and enthusiasm. Perhaps your vision is to have optimistic and positive children, for instance. Does the way you wake them up in the morning evangelize that vision? Are you cheerful and upbeat when you start to rouse them? Or is the first sound they hear panic, annoyance, and the message that they're already late and they haven't even begun the day yet?

How do you evangelize your work vision to your boss? I wrote weekly reports to my AOL boss that marketed my achievements and value to the department. Photocopies of thank-you letters for a job well done should be forwarded to your boss. Notice what areas your boss is overcommitted in (perhaps a too-full speaking schedule?) and volunteer to take some of that load off her shoulders. Don't worry that you might get "scut" work dumped on you. That may happen at first, but at least you're doing work that gets you one step closer to your goal. And once you've demonstrated that you're willing to do what it takes, you'll probably get better assignments.

Don't just limit your marketing efforts vertically to your boss; evangelize yourself to other departments as well. Introduce yourself to the heads of other departments in a low-key, no-pressure way. Say "hi" at the coffee maker. Attend interdepartmental meetings, as inane as you might think they are. Forward articles of interest to other company employees with a note attached explaining exactly why this article made you think of them and how you think they would be interested. In all these situations, come up with one or two sentences marketing you and listen for ways to tie their interests to yours.

Be sure to market your vision externally as well. Join the key associations that represent your profession and your marketplace and become a regular at their meetings. As time allows, be active in special interest groups (SIGs) attached to these organizations. You might find a women's leadership SIG, a technical SIG, or a marketing SIG, and most associations have some sort of newcomer SIG and student chapters. The greater your outside circle of influence, the broader your market will be. And, in turn, the better you will understand the marketplace you're serving.

STRATEGY 4: GET ME A DATE (WITH MINI-DATES IN BETWEEN)!

Bodacious companies and bodacious women give themselves dates by which they want to have certain goals achieved. This is beneficial in a number of ways:

* A time line gives you deadlines to shoot for.

* A time line also helps you break down the task into doable, less intimidating segments. You can go to bed at night satisfied, fulfilled, and happy that you met the day's goal, knowing that you're closer to achieving the big mission.

* The process of designing the time line helps you think through all the external factors that might conflict with or benefit your deadlines. Just as you might coordinate your summer vacation with the dates when school is out, you can also coordinate sitting down to writing your book or moving into an easy-care condo.

* The time line helps you make sure you have plenty of time to get the goal done well. Remember the moment when I discovered I only had a few weeks to prepare for my GREs, after I had been out of school for ten years? Time lines will help you avoid those unpleasant and unhealthy panics.

* Time lines will also give you milestones to celebrate. Don't skip this important step, even if it's just a family spaghetti dinner to celebrate a long day taking the GREs. Celebrations aren't self-indulgent, and they don't have to be extravagant (unless of course you spring for expensive leather jackets for everyone on your team). Celebrations are an important part of your business plan because they remind you and your team how much you depend on them to realize a vision that requires everyone's dedication. Parties, however small, provide an opportunity for everyone to share fun times, the necessary glue that keeps the team together during the more challenging times.

STRATEGY 5: FIGURE OUT HOW TO GET FUNDING

Almost any bodacious ambition involves money somehow. Obviously, companies must consider their budgets when taking on new endeavors. You're no different. You're a start-up, too. Budgets help you just as time lines do. They're not there to remind you over and over again how much you lack. They're there to guide you in determining how much you have to work with. Design a realistic budget that works for you, and you will have all the money you need to see you through to realizing your vision.

You want to make sure you have the money in the first place, of course. Bodacious start-ups know that most of the original investment of effort, time, and money must come from them. But with luck you might be able to attract investors who will help you increase your operating budget to keep your vision alive. Depending on what you're doing and who you know, an investor could be a mate who is willing to be the primary breadwinner while you scale back to focus on a non–revenue-generating goal. Or it could be your company's human resource department that has tuition reimbursement or daycare subsidy program. It could even be the research and development department of your company, if your vision may benefit the company's bottom line. Or perhaps it's a business associate—a customer or a vendor (but watch out for conflicts of interest there)—or a grant from a company that sees the public relations value in supporting your endeavor. Or simply someone you meet at a Chamber of Commerce networking reception.

Again, I can't be all-inclusive here. I am just giving you basic guidelines for developing your personal business plan.

STRATEGY 6: ASK "THE HELP" TO BE A PART OF "THE MANAGEMENT"

Companies want to make sure they have access to employees who can help them achieve their business goals. Although you may not have employees, you certainly have human resources. You're surrounded by resources and support that will help you reach your goals and take care of your life while you're investing in your future vision.

* Your husband, who agrees to cook the meals, and your kids, who agree to wash the dishes, while you hole up in your room studying for law school.

* Your friends, most of whom are probably experts in some aspects of running a business or achieving goals.

* Colleagues and associates who are willing to act on an advisory capacity, as a board of directors might.

* "Janitorial" staff—your kids? a weekly housekeeper?—to keep your environment pleasant and uncluttered so you can concentrate and have time to dedicate to your mission.

STRATEGY 7: WATER THE PLANT

No, I'm not talking about the Swedish ivy that refuses to bloom in the corner. I'm talking about your physical plant: the personal building in which you conduct your business, more commonly called your body.

Companies know how important to staff morale and productivity it is to have a workplace that is safe, well-lit, attractive, and comfortable. Your physical health is your primary work environment. What kind of condition is it in? Is it regularly inspected? Does the furnace work? Can you see clearly out the windows? How's the "curb appeal"?

As the bodacious start-up you are not only the CEO but also the building super. You are also the building itself. Keep the plant running, fix the worrisome conditions that won't get better by themselves. Make sure that both the outside and the inside accurately reflect your overall philosophy of excellence. This doesn't mean you have to be cover-girl gorgeous, sleek, and gleaming like San Francisco's TransAmerica Building. Even funky industrial lofts are attractive. But this does mean that everything about you, inside and out, should accurately broadcast just how bodacious you are. Whether you're a bodacious skyscraper in San Francisco or a bodacious artist's loft in New York's SoHo district at heart, your windows are clean and your varnish gleams.

Be sure to include security in your building maintenance plan. You're not being paranoid to worry about your physical safety. Worldwide, violence against women is the leading cause of death, more common than any of the cancers or heart disease. But even though you may never have been physically attacked, violence still touches your life. Maybe a friend or a family member has been a violence victim. Maybe you have had too many arguments with your daughter about staying out too late. Maybe you choose not to go to concerts or nightclubs alone because navigating through the city late at night makes you feel too vulnerable. You're smart to be cautious, but you can also take steps to increase your safety and expand the boundaries of your bodacious enterprise.

Businesses have security guards, card keys, identification badges, and sprinkler systems. How secure is your plant? Do you feel safe? What systems or services do you need to install so that you feel free to build your bodacious life without looking over your shoulder all the time? Should you (can you) move to a safer neighborhood?

How about taking a self-defense course to help you be more confident? Is the employee parking lot at your company securely lit at night? Will the security guards walk you to your car if you're feeling uneasy for any reason? If you decide to take bodacious action and encourage your company to improve its own security, you can find information at the American Society for Industrial Security (www. asisonline.org).

Achieving the Bodacious Goal: Like No One You've Ever Seen Before

If you've been following your personal business plan, you have been noticing and celebrating your milestone achievements along the way. But what do you do when you're really, thoroughly, and completely done?

You do what bodacious companies do. You assess your current situation and create even more new bodacious visions for the future: Now Economy You Version 3.0.

What's the difference between then and now? You're no longer afraid. You're no longer overwhelmed. You're no longer victimized. You're no longer stuck or lost.

You're bodacious!

Life's Short, Learn Fast

THE JOURNEY to bodaciousness takes courage. It's a process that has many rewarding—as well as retrenching—experiences like the ones I've shared. It involves staring your fears about yourself, about others, about life, in the face. You may wonder sometimes whether you can stay on this road. You will also feel more alive than ever before and know you can't turn back. As you press on, one foot in front of the other, you will mysteriously receive strength to become the Bodacious Woman you want to be. Don't give up. Life's too short; learn as fast as you can.

When I started with AOL I wasn't bodacious, but when we got done with each other this was what we created. I continue to be grateful for the experiences I had there and that I had the privilege to be a small part of creating one of the most influential media of our time. Since leaving AOL I've applied my bodaciousness to venture into new territory, including completing my master's degree in organization development, becoming an angel investor in the human resources technology and consulting company HumanR, and setting out to write this book. Sometimes I wonder who is this adventurous person living inside my body; then I realize I'm just getting more used to my new skin.

The Now Economy isn't a fad; it's here to stay. And with all its topsy-turvy changes and curves, which seem to affect every area of our lives, it's also egging on all the good girls, all the successful women, and all those who feel defeated to be in charge of our lives as never before. Far more than a whisper but not quite yet a scream, it's saying, "Decide who you want to be and go for it. Look within. Think strategically. Act bodaciously. And love every minute of it!"

Bodacious Ways

* Bodacious women don't take it personally.

* Bodacious women thrive on shift and change.

* Bodacious women master office politics.

* Bodacious women focus on what's going right.

* Bodacious women welcome risk.

* Bodacious women give credit where it's due.

* Bodacious women respect themselves.

* Bodacious women have the courage to make tough decisions.

* Bodacious women do not tolerate abuse.

* Bodacious women don't overexplain, don't overcomplain.

* Bodacious women are there.

* Bodacious women don't jump to negative conclusions.

* Bodacious women don't wait to be asked.

* Bodacious women market themselves, their choices, and their achievements.

* Bodacious women see possibilities, not barriers.

* Bodacious women resist negative or victim thinking.

* Bodacious women know their worth.

Recommended Reading

Sarah Ban Breathnach, *Simple Abundance: A Daybook of Comfort and Joy*, New York: Warner, 1995.

William Bridges, *Managing Transitions: Making the Most of Change.* New York: Addison Wesley, 1991.

Richard Carlson, *Don't Worry, Make Money: Spiritual and Practical Ways to Create Abundance and More Fun in Your Life.* New York: Hyperion, 1998.

Henry Cloud and John Townsend, *Boundaries: When to Say Yes, When to Say No, to Take Control of Your Life.* Grand Rapids, Michigan: Zondervan, 1992.

James C. Collins and Jerry I. Porras, *Built to Last: Successful Habits of Visionary Companies*, New York: HarperBusiness, 1997.

Stephen Covey, *The 7 Habits of Highly Effective People: Powerful Lessons in Personal Change.* New York: Simon & Schuster, 1990.

Martha Finney and Deborah Dasch, *Find Your Calling, Love Your Life.* New York: Simon & Schuster, 1998.

Laura Berman Fortgang, *Take Yourself to the Top: The Secrets of America's #1 Career Coach.* New York: Warner Books, 1998.

Pat Heim, *Hardball for Women: Winning at the Game of Business.* New York: Penguin, 1993.

Carole Hyatt and Linda Gottlieb, *When Smart People Fail: Rebuilding Yourself for Success.* New York: Penguin, 1993.

Laurie Beth Jones, *The Path: Creating Your Mission Statement for Work and for Life.* New York: Hyperion, 1997.

Kevin Kelly, *New Rules for the New Economy: 10 Radical Strategies for a Connected World.* New York: Viking, 1999.

Christiane Northrop, *Women's Bodies, Women's Wisdom: Creating Physical and Emotional Health and Healing*, New York: Bantam Doubleday Dell, 1998.

Harriet Rubin, *The Princessa: Machiavelli for Women.* New York: Bantam Doubleday Dell, 1998.

Linda Tschirhart Sanford and Mary Ellen Donovan, *Women & Self-Esteem: Understanding and Improving the Way We Think and Feel About Ourselves.* New York: Penguin, 1985.

Karen Salmansohn, *How to Succeed in Business Without a Penis*, New York: Random House, 1997.

SARK, *The Bodacious Book of Succulence: Daring to Live Your Succulent Wild Life!* New York: Simon & Schuster, 1998.

SARK, *Succulent Wild Woman: Dancing with Your Wonder-Full Self!* New York: Simon & Schuster, 1997.

Martin E. P. Seligman, *Learned Optimism: How to Change Your Mind and Your Life.* New York: Simon & Schuster, 1998.

Barbara Sher, *I Could Do Anything If I Only Knew What It Was: How to Discover What You Really Want and How to Get It.* New York: Dell, 1995.

Kara Swisher, *aol.com: How Steve Case Beat Bill Gates, Nailed the Netheads, and Made Millions in the War for the Web.* New York: Random House, 1999.

Kate White, *9 Secrets of Women Who Get Everything They Want.* New York: Random House, 1999.

- -

Technical Notes

The writing of *Bodacious* was a bicoastal project, with Mary in Virginia and Martha in California.

All notes, files, drafts, chapters, and encouraging e-mails were transmitted via AOL.

- -

Index

advice, 221–222, 228
alliances, 82–85
apologies, 115, 194
appearance, 191–192, 218
assertiveness, 91–94, 196–197

balance, 223–224
barriers, 48–49, 216
behaviors
    for change, 121–125
    knowledge of, 172–173
    masculine, 102–104
blame, 125
bodaciousness
    definition, 24–25, 201
    implementing, 202–203
    see also business plan
    inner emotions, 30–31
    rewards, 27–31, 183–198
    summary, 233–234
body image, 191–192
body language, 113
boundaries, 91–101
bragging, 32, 104
brainstorming, 88
business plan, personal, 202–203,
    208–217

career, 129–130, 218–219
change
    and associates, 64
    and consultants, 85
    and growth, 121–125
    launching, 125–134
    and risk, 50
    and shift, 117–118
    valued behaviors, 121–125
clients, 62–65

commitment, 124
communication, 114, 124, 138,
    196–197
    of objective, 224–226
community relations, 80–81
compensation, 10, 32, 84, 86,
    147–152
competition, 52–53, 74, 109–110
    for current job, 211–212
    of employer, 211
    and job interviews, 142–143
complaints, handling, 114–116
composure, 125
compromise, 178
conclusions, jumping to, 36–38,
    122
confidence, 103–104, 113
confidentiality, 79, 88
conflict, 88, 91–95
confrontation, 105–108, 114–115
consulting, 83–85, 139, 140–141
control, 94–101, 188, 197–198
coping, 89
courage, 124–125
creativity, 48–49, 173
credit, 88, 124, 189–191
crises, 125
criticism, 6, 32, 188
    of self, 49, 184–185, 217
curiosity, 38–39, 192

decision-making, 35–36, 124–125,
    185–186
defensiveness, 36, 187–188
depression, 47, 218
detachment, 44
discomfort, 127–128
discussion groups, 73–74

disparagement, 20–21, 79
dreams, 192–193

emotions, 29–30, 118, 191–192, 210
empire builders, 78–81
expectations, 63, 84
experts, 38, 111, 171
explanations, 113

favors, 21, 51, 76
fear, 25, 118
feedback, 63, 114
feelings, hurt, 41–48
finances, 110–112, 227–228
   see also compensation
flexibility, 19–20
freelancers, 74
friends
   choosing, 32–33, 64–66, 217–218
   favors for, 21, 51
   gaining and losing, 193–194
   objective viewpoint, 102
   requests for help, 21
   as support, 54–55
   see also relationships
fun, 128–129, 140

goodwill, 79
gossip, 177
graciousness, 178–181
gratitude, 51–52
greed, 204–205
growth, 121–125
guilt, 103, 138, 217

health, 191–192, 228–229
help
   offering, 76–81
   requests for, 21, 51
helplessness, 29, 47
hobbies, 71
humor, sense of, 88
hurt feelings, 41–48

information
   sharing, 63, 89, 124, 140–141
   using, 186–187
initiative, 119–120
inner voices, 27–31, 39–41, 202
innovativeness, 39–41
instincts, 101–102
intuition, 37, 39–41, 104, 125

jobs
   beginning new, 152–155
   change initiation, 119–120
   hunting, 7–9, 138, 221–223
   interviews for, 141–144
   layoff from, 137–141
   leaving, 135–137
   offer evaluation, 144–147
   see also compensation
journal, 41–44, 108–109

knowledge, 86–87, 171–173

language, 112–114
layoffs, 137–141
leadership, 73, 124–125
learning, 86, 192
   from biographies, 220
   from New Economy, 204–207
leveraging, 131–134, 221–222
listening, 84
lobbying, 177–178
loneliness, 20–21
loss, 50, 53
luck, 217–220

marketing, 224–226
market overview, 212–213
materialism, 71
men, behaviors of, 102–104
mentors, 55
milestones, 227
mistakes, 88, 125, 204–207

negative comments, 103

negative situations, 89
negative words, 103
negativity, 36–38, 46–48,
    184–185, 188
negotiating, 147–152
networking, 53–56, 74, 79–81,
    122, 222–223
New Economy, 204–207
"no", saying, 93, 103, 195
Now Economy, 22–24
    career paths, 129–130
    and change, 117–118, 186
    job interviews, 141–144
    and relationships, 53–54, 61
    and women, 10–12, 33–34

objectives, 184, 192–193,
    202–203, 214–215
obsessing, 46–48
offense, taking, 41–48
office politics, 159–168
    strategies for, 168–181
office space, 166–168
opinions, 38–39, 188
opportunities
    from disappointments, 56–57
    evaluating, 144–147
    for growth, 119–120
    in workplace, 37–38, 119–120,
    127
optimism, 49, 79, 89
organizations
    knowledge of, 171–172
    professional, 55, 70, 140, 222
outsiders, 130–131

paranoia, 36–38
perfectionism, 49
performance, building on, 85
persistence, 7, 20
personal coaches, 222
perspective, 130–131
physical contact, 165–166
physical fitness, 184, 191–192
pioneering, 18–19

planning, 206–207
platform, 175–177
politics, 159–168
    strategies, 168–181
position, 173–174
positive mindset, 49, 79, 89
power, 98, 165–166
    and self-esteem, 174–175
    types of, 171–174
    see also aggregations
praise, 114
principles, 89, 91–101
    see also stand
professional oganizations, 55, 70,
    140, 222
public service, 72

questions, 84, 142–144
quitting, 135–137, 179–181

records, keeping, 108–109
relationships, 41–48
    acquisitions, 86–87
    aggregations, 85–86
    alliances, 82–85
    as client, 62–65
    and crises, 125
    to discard, 65
    dislike, 109–110
    diverse, 88
    E-Mail, 220
    hierarchical, 219
    and luck, 217–220
    networking, 52–56
    as power, 174
    strategic, 122
    and taking a stand, 105–108, 116
    using, 228
    in workplace, 78–81, 153–155
    see also friends
relevance, 187
reputation, 87–89, 93, 173
resentment, 41–48
resignations, 135–137, 179–181
responsibility, 53

risk, 22, 38, 50, 194–195
  of letting go, 189
  of taking stand, 78
rules, breaking, 196

safety, 229–230
secrets, 79
selectivity, 71
self, responsibility to, 53
self, vision for, 214–217
self awareness, 186–187
self-confidence, 103–104, 113
self criticism, 49, 184–185, 217
self-discovery, 69
self-esteem, 31–33, 72, 174–175,
    184–185
  and credit, 189–191, 218
  and layoffs, 137–141
self improvement, 218
self-respect, 88, 191–192
serendipity, 56–57
sharing
  after layoff, 140–141
  credit, 88, 124
  fun, 128–129
  information, 63, 89, 124
  and power, 165
  of vision, 113–114, 124
shifting, 117–118
skills, 86–87
stand
  and office politics, 175–177
  reactions to, 105–108
  taking, 94–104
start-ups, 16–21
stock options, 149–152
strategic behavior, 122, 184–186,
    192–193
  for implementation, 220–230
  and politics, 168–181
strategic business units, 223–224
stress, 127–128

success factors, 215
survival habits, 188–189

tenacity, 20
time, 53–54, 86, 223–224
time line, 226–227
touch, 165–166
transitions, 117–118, 127–123,
    131–134
trustworthiness, 97–99

uncertainty, 128

value, knowing, 33–34
vendors, 62–65, 71
victimization, 29
visibility, 130–131, 220
vision, 214–217, 224–226
volunteering, 72, 79, 80–81, 177

winning, 169–171
women
  feelings, 15–16
  inner voices, 27–31, 39–41
  in Now Economy, 10–12,
    33–34
  relationships with, 13, 55
  as start-ups, 16–21
  in TV commercials, 13–15
workplace group for, 73
workplace
  after layoffs, 138
  in business plan, 211–212
  communication projects, 79–80
  and depression, 47–48
  leadership group, 73
  opportunities in, 37–38,
    119–120, 127
  and personal life, 120
  politics in, 159–168
  relationships in, 78–81,
    153–155

About the Authors

MARY E. FOLEY

At age 33, Mary E. Foley retired independently wealthy from America Online, where she started ten years earlier as an eight-dollar-per-hour customer service representative. Currently, she shares her message as an author, speaker, and personal coach through her company, Bodacious! Ventures, LLC. In addition, she serves on the board of HumanR, a human resources software and consulting company for which she became an angel investor. Parts of her story have appeared in *Kiplinger's Personal Finance*, *Fast Company*, and *Across the Board* magazines. She holds a bachelor's degree in industrial engineering from Virginia Tech and a master's degree in organization development from Pepperdine University. She lives in Reston, Virginia, and can be contacted at www.gobodacious.com.

MARTHA I. FINNEY

Martha I. Finney is the author of *Find Your Calling, Love Your Life* (Simon & Schuster, 1998) and producer of *Working from the Heartland*, a Web site documentary exploring joy in the American workplace. Internationally recognized as a leading authority in self-actualization through work, she helps companies retain and rededicate valued employees. She has appeared on CNN and NPR and in major newspapers throughout the United States. She lives in Northern California and can be reached at MarthaFinn@aol.com.